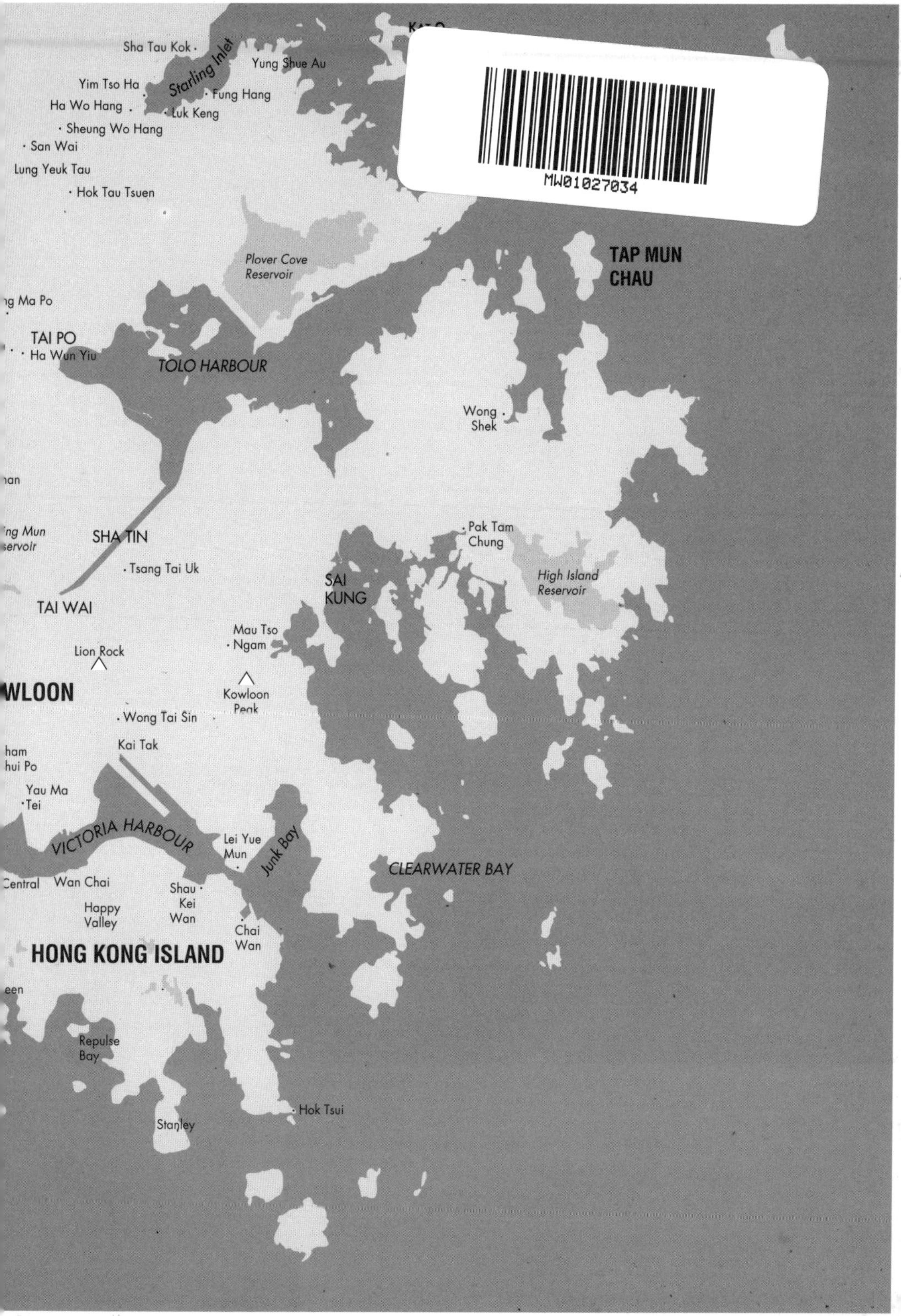

Sha Tau Kok

Starling Inlet

Yung Shue Au

Yim Tso Ha
Ha Wo Hang
Fung Hang
Luk Keng
Sheung Wo Hang
San Wai
Lung Yeuk Tau
Hok Tau Tsuen

KAT O

TAP MUN CHAU

Plover Cove Reservoir

ng Ma Po

TAI PO
Ha Wun Yiu

TOLO HARBOUR

Wong Shek

han

ng Mun servoir

SHA TIN
Tsang Tai Uk

Pak Tam Chung

High Island Reservoir

SAI KUNG

TAI WAI

Lion Rock

Mau Tso Ngam

WLOON

Kowloon Peak

Wong Tai Sin

Kai Tak

ham hui Po

Yau Ma Tei

VICTORIA HARBOUR

Lei Yue Mun

Junk Bay

CLEARWATER BAY

Central   Wan Chai

Shau Kei Wan

Happy Valley

Chai Wan

HONG KONG ISLAND

een

Repulse Bay

Hok Tsui

Stanley

DISCOVERING HONG KONG'S CULTURAL HERITAGE

DISCOVERING
Hong Kong's Cultural Heritage

By
PATRICIA LIM

With photographs and illustrations by
ANTONIA MYATT
and
PATRICIA LIM

HONG KONG
OXFORD UNIVERSITY PRESS
OXFORD   NEW YORK
1997

Oxford University Press

Oxford New York
Athens Auckland Bangkok Bogota Bombay
Buenos Aires Calcutta Cape Town Dar es Salaam
Delhi Florence Hong Kong Istanbul Karachi
Kuala Lumpur Madras Madrid Melbourne
Mexico City Nairobi Paris Singapore
Taipei Tokyo Toronto

and associated companies in
Berlin Ibadan

Oxford is a trade mark of Oxford University Press

First published 1997
This impression (lowest digit)
1 3 5 7 9 10 8 6 4 2

Published in the United States
by Oxford University Press, New York

British Library Cataloguing in Publication Data
available

Library of Congress Cataloging-in-Publication data
Lim, Patricia
Discovering Hong Kong's cultural heritage. / by Patricia Lim; with photographs
and illustrations by Antonia Myatt.
p. cm.
Includes bibliographical references and index.
ISBN 0-19-590075-8
1. New Territories (China)—Civilization. 2. New Territories (China)—'
Tours. I. Title.
DS796.H76N485 1997
915.12504'6—DC21 97-29015
CIP

Printed in Hong Kong
Published by Oxford University Press (China) Ltd
18/F Warwick House, Taikoo Place, 979 King's Road,
Quarry Bay, Hong Kong

*I dedicate this book to my family who have given me
so much help and support, and, in particular, to my long-suffering
husband who has accompanied me on so many
expeditions over the years.*

Patricia Lim is a Cambridge graduate with a degree in history. She has worked in England, Switzerland, and Singapore, and moved to Hong Kong in the 1970s. In Hong Kong, she has taught at the Hong Kong Polytechnic University and the French International School.

FOREWORD
by Lady Pamela Youde

Most new arrivals in Hong Kong expect to see a lively modern city full of stylish high-rise architecture and exciting shops. Few of them realize that behind the glittering facade lie beautiful historic buildings and spectacular countryside.

Finding these out-of-the-way places has often proved daunting, but now Patricia Lim shows how easy it is when you know how. Using her deep knowledge of the local history and cultural background of Hong Kong, she paints a vivid picture of the ancestors of the people who throng the streets, and takes us to explore the villages that many of them came from not so long ago.

With the help of excellent maps and photographs, all who wish to see something of the real Hong Kong can set off with confidence to the remotest sites. With Patricia Lim as their guide they can be sure of a fascinating and rewarding day.

Pamela Youde

ACKNOWLEDGEMENTS

I would like to acknowledge the great debt I owe to all those members of the Royal Asiatic Society whose research published in the *Royal Asiatic Journal* I have found invaluable, and whose lectures have kindled the interest that led me to write this book. In particular I would like to thank Dr James Hayes for his kindness in taking time to read the manuscript and Mr Tse Shun Kai for the elegant scholarly calligraphy he has contributed to this book. I would also like to thank the Antiquities and Monuments Office and the Director of the Cultural Division, Mr Chiu Siu-tsan, and his assistant, Miss S. Siu, for the encouragement, they gave me. I am particularly grateful to the many residents of the villages who over the past twenty years have never failed to show me kindness and treat my enquiries with patience. Their friendliness has added greatly to the very real pleasure my visits have given me. Finally I would like to thank all those at Oxford University Press who have worked to make this book successful and in particular Rebecca Lloyd for the hours of free time she has spent personally testing out the routes, and for her excellent suggestions and editing skills. The maps are by Mr Ricky Wong To Ngai. Tony Cheng of Scientific Photo Company gave me valuable support and help with the photography.

The photograph of the Taoists in the second plate section is reproduced by kind permission of Ian Robinson. The picture of Confucius lecturing in the second plate section is reproduced with the kind permission of the Qufu Administrative Commission of the Cultural Relics of Shandong. I would like to thank Mr H. S. Chui for the photograph he contributed on page 40 (top right).

CONTENTS

NOTE ON CHINESE NAMES

There are several systems for romanizing Chinese words. For Cantonese spellings I have used the common romanizations used in Hong Kong. Words taken from Mandarin Chinese (Putonghua) have been romanized using the pinyin system. However, for clarity, in some cases I have used the most common romanization of particular words. Some equivalent spellings are given as examples below.

Pinyin	Wade-Giles or other form
Dao, Daoism	Tao, Taoism.
Daodejing	Tao Te Ching
Qing Dynasty	Ch'in / Ching Dynasty
Tang Dynasty	T'ang Dynasty
Song Dynasty	Sung Dynasty
Zhou Dynasty	Chou Dynasty
Huang Di (the Yellow Emperor)	Huang Ti / Hwang Ti
Laozi	Lao Tzu / Lao Tze
Taijiquan	t'ai chi ch'uan
Yijing	I Ching

INTRODUCTION

When you compare Hong Kong with other great cities of the world, it is not grand with castles or cathedrals, nor is the cultural heritage easily and readily accessible as it is elsewhere. Well-known tourist attractions in other countries usually have a full complement of guided or self-guiding tours, richly illustrated potted histories, excellent, artistic picture postcards, and souvenirs of all kinds. When I visited Hong Kong's Ten Thousand Buddha Temple, a group of international tourists expressed great disappointment at the lack of tourist literature, except for one poorly photocopied sheet. Even the packs of postcards on sale looked twenty years out of date.

This is one example of the inaccessibility of Hong Kong's many historical and cultural sights, thus making sight-seeing tiring and frustrating—especially in the heat of summer—encouraging tourists to give up and label Hong Kong a cultural desert. Furthermore, when people go sight-seeing in their own countries it is much easier for them to relate to what they see. But the foreigner in Hong Kong lacks the cultural background and thus much of Hong Kong's deep underlying heritage is missed. In order to discover more than what is superficially presented, one must be a different sort of tourist and look at what is embedded in the everyday life of the people, as well as in its monuments.

In this book I have tried to uncover and present a way of seeing Hong Kong which will lead to a deeper understanding of its Chinese heritage. To best explain the cultural heritage of each landmark, I have provided a description, and, where appropriate, some historical background, and how it now features in the present-day lives of the people.

It is easy to get lost in the New Territories. It would be helpful, before embarking on the trips in Part 2, to buy the new editions of the 'Countryside Series' maps, published by the Map Office. You can buy them in bookshops, as well as from the Map Office itself on the fourteenth floor of the Murray Building, just below the Peak Tram Terminal on Garden Road. The maps show many places of interest which are numbered. I have included the numbers in the text wherever they occur.

PART 1

Cultural Heritage

CHAPTER 1

HONG KONG PEOPLE

Newcomers to Hong Kong are apt to think of Chinese people as a homogeneous group, unaware of the many different groups of people from diverse provinces all over China who make up the population of Hong Kong.

But even more important to understanding the background of Hong Kong and the New Territories is the divide between the Cantonese-speaking settlers: the Punti, who arrived from the tenth century onwards and who colonized the fertile valleys; and the late-coming Hakka who began to settle during the late seventeenth century and had to make do with the less-productive hilly land—they have thus never been as prosperous nor had the same prestige. The difference between these two groups is stressed by the two completely different dialects which are mutually incomprehensible. The Hakka dialect is a northern dialect, thought to be very close to the original Mandarin before it was coloured by the language of the Mogul and the Manchu people.

The boat people form a third important group. They can be divided into the local Tanka people who arrived in Hong Kong probably well before the Punti, and the Hoklo who came to Hong Kong in the nineteenth century from the region of Swatow. The Hoklo wear wide conical hats, while the Tanka people—whose name means

Hoklo hat (left) and Tanka hat

CHINESE DYNASTIES

Legendary Period (Prehistoric Era)
Mythical Sage-emperors
Fu Xi, inventor of the trigram
Shen Nung, the father of Chinese
medicine (c. 2838 BC)
Huang Di, the Yellow Emperor, the
father of agriculture.

Xia Dynasty (c. 2100–1600 BC)
Yu, mythical emperor, who stopped
floods

Shang Dynasty (c. 1600–1027 BC)
Fine bronzes appear
Silk is used
Ox bone and tortoiseshell used for
divination

Zhou Dynasty (c. 1027–256 BC)
I Ching, the Book of Changes,
compiled
The Golden Age of Philosophy
Confucius (c. 551–479 BC)
Laozi (sixth century BC)
Tao Te Ching compiled
Spring and Autumn period
(722–481 BC)
Warring States Period (475–221 BC)

Qin Dynasty (221–207 BC)
China united
Chinese script, weights and measures
standardized
Great Wall begun (214 BC)

Han Dynasty (206 BC–AD 220)
Beginnings of paper making
Confucianism established as the
official religion
Buddhism enters China by the Silk
Road
Hong Kong Region incorporated into
China
Construction of Lei Cheng Uk Tomb,
Sham Shui Po

The Three Kingdoms (AD 220–80)
Rise of Buddhism

Jin Dynasty (265–420)

Northern and Southern Dynasties (420–589)

Sui Dynasty (581–618)
Confucian system of Civil Service
Examinations introduced

Tang Dynasty (618–907)
China reunified
Great achievements in poetry,
sculpture, and painting
Suppression of Buddhist Monasteries
Rise of the Scholar Civil Servant

Five Dynasties and Ten Kingdoms (907–979)
First military use of gunpowder

CHINESE DYNASTIES

Song Dynasty (960–1279)
Tang Fu Yip settles his family in
Hong Kong
Genghis Khan and his Mongol
army invade China
Song Princess puts herself under
Tang protection, 1129

Yuan Dynasty (1271–1368)
The boy Song emperors take
refuge in Kowloon and Lantau,
1275–1279
Song's last stand is defeated
Mongol Dynasty established by
Kublai Khan
Visit of Marco Polo

Ming Dynasty (1368–1644)

Qing Dynasty (1644–1911)
Established by the Manchu
Clearance Order of the Coastal
Region including Hong Kong,
1662
Treaty of Nanking—cession of
Hong Kong to Britain, 1843
Convention of Peking—cession of
Kowloon, 1860
Bubonic Plague hits Hong Kong,
1894
Cession of the New Territories,
1898

Republic of China (1912–1949)

People's Republic of China (1949–)

'egg head'—wear deep-brimmed domed hats. The Tanka may be descended from the ancient and shadowy Yue tribes who had their own distinct culture and whose language has influenced Cantonese. Archeological evidence suggests that the coastal areas around Hong Kong have been inhabited by these people since the Neolithic period (c. 4500–1500 BC). The Tanka may be descended from the very earliest inhabitants of Hong Kong.

Like the Hakka, the boat people were formerly despised and discriminated against. They were not allowed to intermarry nor to sit for the Civil Service Examination. It was only in the reign of Kangxi (1662–1722) that they were allowed to build shacks for themselves on the water's edge and live ashore.

Now only a few live entirely on their boats as they used to, but they still congregate on the islands and in distinctive fishing villages such as Tai O or on the island of Cheung Chau. A number of boat people still use their knowledge of the sea to make their living by mariculture—operating rafts with sunken nets in which fish fry are kept until they have reached marketable size. They are also involved in deep-sea fishing and selling a whole range of dried sea products to local visitors. In Tai O or on the outer islands these products can be seen drying in the sun on flat rattan trays.

The territory of Hong Kong was very much a backwater in the history of China. It first became part of the

Chinese empire when the army of the Qin emperor, Qin Shi Huang Di conquered the Yue people in 214 BC. The only monument to this time is the Han tomb, now a museum, at Lei Cheng Uk, Sham Shui Po, which was discovered by workmen in 1955. It was propably built for a Chinese officer attached to the local garrison. A total of fifty-eight bronze and pottery items were found including models of houses, granaries, wells, a stove, cooking vessels, and a bronze mirror.

Only two events made a real impact on the territory. Both involved the downfall of a dynasty to northern invaders. The first occurred during the overthrow of the Song dynasty by the Mongols. In 1276 the Song court fled to Guangdong by boat leaving behind the emperor, Gong Di, in enemy hands. Any hope of resistance centred on two young princes, Gong Di's brothers. The older boy, Di Zheng, aged nine, was declared emperor, and, in 1277, the imperial court sought refuge first in Silvermine Bay (Mui Wo) on Lantau Island and later in Kowloon Walled City (now demolished). The Sung Wong Toi rock carving near Kai Tak is thought to date from their six-month stay there. The older brother became ill and died, and was succeeded by the younger, Di Bing, aged seven. When in 1279 the Song army was defeated in its last battle against the Mongols in the Pearl River Delta, a high official is said to have taken the boy emperor in his arms and jumped from a clifftop into the sea drowning both of them. An

official from the court of the young emperors gave Hong Kong one of its most popular gods, Hau Wong (see page 77)

The communal meal *poon choi*, literally 'basin food', served in villages to celebrate important occasions, is also thought to have originated at this time. Circular tables, each seating twelve people, are set up, and each is supplied with a metal basin filled to capacity with all kinds of food. The lowest level is made up of vegetables, followed by bean curd, and mushrooms. This is topped by squid, several kinds of pork and chicken, and the basin may be crowned with fresh prawns. This type of feast is said to have originated at a time when villagers filled tubs and basins with the best food they could muster to offer to the young emperor and his court who were taking refuge in their midst.

The second event happened in the aftermath of the overthrow of the Ming dynasty by the Manchu. Piratical fleets, under the leadership of Koxinga and, after his death, of his family members, remained loyal to the Ming dynasty and continued to defy the authority of the Manchu rulers. This led to the drastic action known as *Ts'in Fuk* or the 'Great Clearance' in the spring of 1662. The Manchu emperor, Kangxi, ordered that the population of Guangdong and Fujian provinces move first fifty *li* (about twenty-five kilometres), and then another thirty *li* inland, and a scorched-earth policy was put into effect in an attempt to starve

A 'basin meal' celebrating the reopening of the village temple at Wang Chau

out the rebels. No relief was given to the villagers who lost their homes and livelihood. But in 1669 the provincial Mandarins, Chou Yau Tak and Wong Loi Yam, managed to persuade the emperor to reverse his edict, allowing the villagers to return to their devastated homelands and rebuild their lives. These two men are said to have died battling bandits and achieved supernatural powers. They are revered to this day in temples and study halls around the region. It is recorded that about 16,000 people were driven from their homes during the Great Clearance, but only 1,648 of them are said to have returned. In 1669 a district magistrate reported that when he arrived in the region he found many of the old people and children lying dead in ditches after dying of hunger. It took the local clans many years to recover and rebuild their economic strength after such a tragedy. The depopulation was so great that the Hakka were encouraged to come to work the land left vacant and untilled.

CHAPTER 2

VILLAGE LIFE

Throughout Hong Kong, but particularly in the New Territories and outlying islands, there are many interesting old villages where local life has changed very little over the generations, maintaining many of its beliefs and traditions. The traditional villagers, in the days when rice was grown and the fields were intensively cultivated, were a tough, ingenious, self-sufficient people. Up until about the 1960s these communities grew their own food, made their own clothes, doctored their own illnesses, and built their own houses. In the autumn of 1926, the village elders entertained Sir Cecil Clementi, then governor, to a banquet at Tai Po. The special feature of this banquet was that all the ingredients of every dish were home grown except for the shark's fin soup. Mr Schofield, a district officer attending the banquet, remembers the air bladders of sargassum seaweed as being particularly tasty.

The names of the villages all have meanings, often giving a geographical description of the site. Opposite is a list of the more usual Cantonese words that are found in local place-names. As you approach any of these villages you may notice that they have been very similarly planned, forming straight lines

Food drying, Luk Keng

PLACE-NAMES

The following are the meanings of some of the more common elements that make up local place-names:-

Directions

Pak	North
Nam	South
Tung	East
Sai	West
Sheung	Upper
Ha	Lower

Village

Heung	A number of linked villages
Tsuen	Village
Uk	Family settlement
Wai	Walled village

Buildings

Hui	Market
Miu	Temple
Kung	Taoist Temple
Lau	House
Tong	Hall
Tsz	Hall

Geographical Features

Au	Pass
Kok	Headland
Shan	Mountain
Shek	Rock
Tin	Field

Wo	Valley
Yuen	Garden

Water

Chung	Stream, estuary
Chau	Island
Hang	Valley, stream
Ho	River
Hoi	Sea
Mun	Channel, passage, gate
Shui	Water
O	Harbour, bay, inlet
Wan	Bay

Others

San	New
Lo	Old
Siu	Small
Tai	Big
Cheung	Long
Lung	Dragon

Yim Tso Ha with its fung shui *wood behind and fields in front*

nestling into a hillside. This follows the rules of *fung shui* or geomancy (see page ¿) which states that villages should preferably face south and look out over water. South is the direction of the divine and powerful. At court only the emperor was allowed to face south: all those around him had to face north. Antique maps of China show south at the top and north at the bottom. From the hills behind flows the *yang* force which gives energy, and the flat fields below the village, with their meandering streams or paths, supply the *yin* force, boosting the local fertility level. The village should ideally be situated where the two forces meet and balance each other. The tree-covered sheltering hill behind protects it from the cold winds and the malignant spirits of the north, as well as from an excessive flow of *yang* force. To the east and west, two tree-covered 'arms' should enfold the village like an armchair. The western 'arm'—which

represents the Azure Dragon—should be higher than the eastern 'arm'—which represents the White Tiger and which is dangerous if not kept in balance. Thus for *fung shui* reasons, woodland behind the village was never cut down. These ancient groves of indigenous trees have been left intact for centuries, with their wildlife undisturbed.

In fact, many aspects of *fung shui* beliefs are common sense. The sheltering trees kept the villages safe from landslips and typhoon winds, and the location above the valley floor meant they were not so susceptible to flooding. Any disturbance to the *fung shui* is potentially serious as it affects the luck and prosperity (not to mention fertility) of the village. An example of this occurred in 1937 at San Shek Wan on Lantau Island, when a typhoon uprooted a number of large trees, leaving great gaps in the *fung shui* protected area of the Hakka village.

8

Following this incident, villagers noticed a distinct drop in the number of male babies being born and blamed the misfortune on the devastation left from the typhoon, which exposed the village to bad spirits. Subsequently, the villagers moved the entire village a quarter of a mile inland, abandoning their homes and ancestral hall.

The magnificent palaces in Beijing, temples and monasteries throughout China, and the smallest hamlets in the New Territories were all built using the same *fung shui* guidelines to ensure harmony with the cosmos.

Around the less modernized villages you will see reminders of the former importance of the rice crop. Where left undisturbed, the old paddy fields stretch out in front of the houses, and if you walk among them you will see the irrigation systems still intact, with narrow concrete channels bringing water to flood the fields. Many of the paddy fields have now been turned into storage parks for containers, or

Village houses, Tap Mun Chau, with rice-drying areas in front

sites for Spanish-style villas. In front of the village houses you can still sometimes see the flat concrete areas which were originally used for drying the rice harvest—essential to prevent the rice from mouldering and becoming inedible.

Up until the middle of this century the two annual rice harvests were essential to the survival of the village. Two failed consecutive harvests meant hardship—belts were tightened, life was grim—until the next harvest. Three failures meant famine and death. The last great famine took place during the Second World War when it is said that the Japanese requisitioned the seed rice, leaving none to be planted. As a consequence, one-third of the population of the New Territories died. Many of the

Old rice terraces, Sheung Wo Hang

9

Rice winnower

hills in the New Territories still show signs of terracing for the hill paddies, which were planted at a different time from the main rice crop. This meant that at least there was the hill rice to fall back on if the main harvest failed.

Tucked away, perhaps in the village clan hall, you may find an old rice winnower. This is a wind machine with a series of paddles in a drum. On the top is the hopper for the rice that has already been threshed in the fields. If the operator was extremely skilful, the wind would blow the grain, the bran, and the chaff into the waiting baskets. The grain would then be exchanged in the market for rice of a poorer quality to feed the family. The bran fed the pigs and the chaff was thrown out for the chickens.

You can often find heavy old quern stones lying abandoned around the villages. These were used for grinding

rice flour for New Year cakes. The quern consisted of two granite drums, the smaller one fitting into the larger and revolving inside it. It was extremely hard work to turn (using a long wooden beam) so the work was usually done by the younger, fitter women. You might also see round, basketware stands containing what look like quern stones, but in fact are made of hardened mud with slivers of bamboo set into them. These were used in the same way as the quern stones, but their purpose was to dehusk the rice to make it edible.

Radiating from the village are narrow pathways connecting the village to the outside world. The newer ones may be concreted, but many of the original tracks still exist, especially in the remoter areas. These are very rough and lined with granite slabs, and are a reminder of the poverty of the area. They were built purely as

Quern stone

10

footpaths, being too narrow and often too steep for horses, or even donkeys. Everything coming into the territory had to be carried on the backs of men or women, usually by means of a bamboo pole across the shoulders from which two baskets were suspended, or, if the load was too heavy, slung between two people.

These footpaths led to the local market town which was the hub of economic activity for the surrounding villages. Such markets as Yuen Long, Shek Wu Hui, Tai Po, Sai Kung, or Kowloon each took place on a different day of the week and gave the villagers a chance to sell their grass, firewood, or fattened pigs in exchange for such necessities as incense sticks, stationery for children at the village school, oil, or kerosene. Often the village could only supply part of its needs in rice and relied on some special activity, such as lime or salt production, or a particular produce to pay for those items not covered by the sale of rice. The market town was also the centre for worship of the gods, with the principal shopkeepers organizing donations for the upkeep of the temple, and the cost of putting on feasts and operas on the birthday of the temple's main god. From these organizations the *kai fongs* or town councils grew up and later began to administer the markets. The *kai fong* meetings were usually held in the temple and the common scales— used for the settlement of disputes concerning weights and measures— were kept there, as they still are, for

Deserted village, Yung Shue Au

instance, at the Man Mo Temple in Tai Po.

Over the last few decades, much of the fertile land in the New Territories has been allowed to lie fallow or become strewn with unsightly car dumps or container parks. Hong Kong's planning laws are insufficient to control this kind of environmental degradation when pitted against against the strength of local interests. For the villagers there is much more money to be made from container parks and the like than from agriculture. Besides, so many young men have left to work overseas or in the towns, that there is a serious shortage of manpower to work the fields.

If you walk in the wilder parts of the New Territories you will notice ruined, deserted villages; in others many houses stand empty and padlocked and only a few are still inhabited by elderly villagers. It is a sad fact that the number of villages is decreasing every decade, especially those far-flung settlements without easy access to public transport.

11

Walled Villages

Entrance to Wai Loi Tsuen, Sheung Shui

Old walled villages can be identified by their names. A walled village will usually have a name ending in *wai* and a village without walls will more likely have a name ending in *tsuen*. Many *wai* still retain interesting reminders of their traditional origins, with gatehouses, watchtowers, walls, or moats clearly visible. These were originally built to defend the inhabitants from intruders.

The gatehouses could easily be defended since the entrances are so narrow that only one person at a time could gain admittance. Sometimes heavy wooden bars slot into a wooden framework to obstruct the way. Elsewhere strong cast-iron gates can be securely locked at night. The village would also have kept a store of weaponry, which accounts for the large number of ancient cannons found in many places around Hong Kong, such as outside Fan Ling Wai and the Tang clan hall at Ha Tsuen Shi.

It is well worth visiting one of the museums of village life. In Tsuen Wan, a short walk from the Mass Transit Railway (MTR) station lies Sam Tung Uk, a 200-year-old Hakka walled village, a good example of a typical clan village, with displays of furnishings and artifacts (see page 138). Just inside the Sai Kung Country Park, Sheung Yiu Village has been turned into a fascinating museum of village life (see page 148).

The protection of the gods was of the utmost importance, particularly when villages were under threat. The village Earth God sits in his shrine inside the gatehouse, protecting the entrance. Inside the village, the main thoroughfare runs from the gatehouse to the small temple that stands guarding the northern perimeter. The closely packed houses are built in double rows, separated by narrow lanes off the main path. Each walled village has its own well or water supply, which was essential for the village to withstand a siege.

Up until recently the larger villages organized and paid for their own watchmen to keep constant guard throughout the night against fire, floods, and thieves or marauders (both of the animal and human kind). The watchmen tendered for the job to the village elders, recouping their expenses by charging a set fee to each household for their services, usually paid in rice. The night was divided into four watches, sounded out on a drum.

You may wonder what the villagers feared so much in the peaceful countryside. Bandits and pirates roamed the countryside, often resorting to rape, pillage, or kidnapping. Quarrels between the clans were also frequent and occasionally led to full-scale warfare.

Pirates and Kidnappers

Many of the walled villages date from the break up of the Ming dynasty and the invasion of the Manchu. In 1644 a misguided general of the declining Ming dynasty allowed the Manchu army to cross the Great Wall of China, resulting in the establishment of the Qing dynasty. The ripples from this event disturbed the peace of the New Territories where Li Wan Jung led a last-ditch attempt to resist the Manchu. It was the brigandage and depredations of his men in the eight years before his capture in 1656 that drove the people of Sheung Shui, and others, to build walls around their villages.

But even after the capture of Li Wan Jung, patriots such as Cheng Kung or Koxinga, as he is better known in the West, continued to threaten the Qing dynasty at sea, with operations stretching from Hainan to Taiwan, and up to 50,000 men at their command. Koxinga and all his family had good reasons for hating the Manchus. They had lured his father with false promises to their headquarters and after making him drunk at a banquet had taken him prisoner and subsequently beheaded him; as a result Koxinga's mother committed suicide.

A number of Koxinga's followers led by a family member, Cheng Kin, made Hong Kong the centre of their activities which were more piratical than patriotic. It was Cheng Kin's grandson, Cheng Yat, who from 1723 onwards held the hills behind Lei Yue Mun with such ferocity that the hill

Koxinga

Pirate ship

where they built their stronghold became known as Devil's Peak. In the early 1800s, Cheng Kin, a descendant of the same Cheng family, and also a pirate, attacked numerous villages in the Hong Kong region, including Ping Shan. When he was killed in action in Vietnam, his wife took over her husband's role of pirate chief and went on to expand the family's power. Besides ruling over a confederation of six fleets, each sailing under a different coloured flag, she regulated the pirates' finances by selling 'passports to sea' (a pass into her protection racket) along the entire South China coastline. In 1809, before her downfall, she commanded between 50,000 and 70,000 people and 1,200 junks.

Another well-known local pirate, Cheung Po Tsai, after being kidnapped at the age of fifteen by the Chengs and learning their 'trade', rose to command a pirate fleet of more than 270 boats and 15,000 men, with hideouts at Stanley and Tung Chung on Lantau. It was he who originally built the Tin Hau temples at Ma Wan, Cheung Chau, and Stanley. These temples continue to be dedicated to fishing and seafaring activities, although they are now more law abiding. Cheung Po Tsai fought and defeated the Imperial Navy several times in 1808, but finally, trapped, surrounded, and isolated, he surrendered, bringing with him his men and junks, as well as 5,000 women, 7,000 swords, and 1,200 guns. In exchange he was offered a post in the Qing military establishment.

Between 1849 and 1850 British sailors of the China station claimed the huge sum of £76,690 as rewards for capturing pirates, causing the British Admiralty to stop paying pirate bounties. In 1850, the last of the powerful pirate bands was suppressed by the combined forces of the British and Manchu navies, and Hong Kong gained the name of Tai Ping Shan— 'Mountain of Peace'. Tai Ping Shan Street, situated just above and parallel to Hollywood Road running west of the Man Mo Temple, is the centre of the oldest residential quarter of Hong Kong Island.

The fact that pirates continued to prey on villages into this century is shown by my own family history. Around 1920, my mother-in-law was kidnapped from a village near the coast of Guangdong as a baby. She never knew her real name or her birthday. She was raised by the pirates and, luckily for her, was befriended by the pirate captain's daughter. As a result she was well treated, and when she reached the marriageable age of thirteen it was arranged for her to become the youngest wife of a man from a respected Fujian family.

The pirates knew no bounds in their lawless activity, and in 1912 they surprised and overpowered the police station on Cheung Chau, killing one of the policemen, and escaping with arms and ammunition. This incident forced the British to build a better defended police station. In 1924 a Cheung Chau ferry was captured by pirates and, in the following year, a ferry was even attacked in Victoria Harbour.

It is said that before the widespread use of motorboats, these later bands of marauders used dragon boats in their attacks, in which the crew would be blindfolded to ensure nothing distracted them from rowing. The helmsman kept the course and the drummer maintained the beat. The dragon boat would pull alongside its prey, whereupon the rowers would tear off their blindfolds, draw knives from their belts, and leap aboard.

Pirates were not the only people to be feared by the villagers at the turn of the century. The large-scale emigration of men from the villages of South China down to Singapore and Malaysia, and westwards to North America, fuelled a lucrative trade in girls for prostitution. Many of these girls were kidnapped and sold to pimps. According to government records from the 1880s the average price paid by overseas Chinese for a good-looking girl aged between sixteen and eighteen was HK$350. At the turn of the century a Chinese San Francisco businessman wrote to his contact in Hong Kong that he would be willing to pay HK$1,000 for two girls if they were from Hong Kong. The Reverend Dr Eitel, in an official memorandum written in 1892, said that: 'the kidnapping of girls especially is so common and a matter of such every day occurrence that in local schools it was a common thing to see girls dressed in boys' clothing. . . . at the street corners offers of reward posted up concerning lost girls is a daily sight.' Boys were not immune from kidnapping gangs either. They would be sold to childless couples desperate for a 'son' to carry on the family name and meet their needs in the afterlife. The young son and daughter of Tsang Koon Man, a prosperous quarry-owner who built the walled village of Tsang Tai Uk in Sha Tin (see page 128), were said to have been kidnapped in the 1850s and returned only after he paid a large ransom.

Inter-clan Hostility

Another threat to village peace came from within in the form of inter-clan hostility, which sometimes flared up into full-scale battles. In one such battle in the 1860s the villagers of Shing Mun (now flooded by the Shing Mun Reservoir) and Tsuen Wan each killed seventeen villagers of the opposing party. A memorial to the dead men of Shing Mun can be seen in the Kwan Ti temple in Kam Tin, and to the Tsuen Wan dead in the Tin Hau temple in, Tsuen Wan (see page 136). The reasons for the hostilities are far from clear, but they may have involved the deeply

resented levies imposed on the Shing Mun villagers' pineapple crop when they crossed Tsuen Wan territory on the way to market. The dam across the Shing Mun Reservoir is called the Pineapple Dam in memory of this trade.

This kind of inter-clan warfare still occasionally breaks out in China. A year or two ago in Guangdong, the *South China Morning Post* reported, a quarrel arose between two clans both of which claimed the right to exploit some caves for tourism. One clan, alleging that the caves fell in their territory, attacked the rival clan with an assortment of weapons, including guns, and a number of deaths ensued.

Thus in the days before telephones and efficient police forces, a small, close-knit community could respond quickly to any threats or dangers, and act as an effective means of security for the village.

CHAPTER 3

VILLAGE HOUSES

Traditional village houses remain in most villages, sandwiched among the smart new villas. Architecturally they have remained virtually the same for thousands of years. The mortise and tenon joinery used to secure the roof rafters is identical to those recently discovered on a site at Hemedin in Zhejiang province that date back to 9000 BC. Pottery houses buried centuries ago with the dead for their use in the underworld hardly differ in shape or layout.

However, these houses are not comfortable to live in. They are hot in summer and cold in winter, and they lack proper foundations which means that they are susceptible to damp. Because of this villagers welcome moving into the new three-storey villas with more modern facilities.

The Exterior

As you look around a village, you may see the few remaining fine old tiled roofs of the older houses with their boat-shaped roof ridges curving upwards at both ends. These are said to represent the tails of swallows. Since the return of the swallows to nest under the eaves was welcomed as an omen of

*Village street,
Luk Keng*

17

approaching success, villagers believed that living under the tail of a swallow would bring success to all who lived in that house.

Houses were built in a rectangle with few very small windows to keep out the hot sun. For the same reason they had thick insulating walls coated with a lime wash that reflects rather than absorbs the sun's rays. The overhanging eaves of the pitched roofs and the moulded plaster panels over doors and windows also block out the sun as well as providing protection from the torrential rains that come with typhoons. These panels are often attractively decorated with painted

Door Gods, couplets at either side, and a mirror above to deter evil spirits, Pak Tin Pa

plaster work of flowers, symbolizing peace, pine trees for longevity, or bats for happiness. Each decorative detail is symbolic, there to ensure the happiness, longevity, and prosperity of the household. The box opposite lists the most important animals, plants, and natural phenomena and what each one symbolizes.

The Doorway

Chinese houses are always symmetrical, with the door placed in the centre and carefully protected from evil influences and bad luck. Hanging from the top of the door you will see five red speckled papers representing the Five Blessings: long life, wealth, health and peace, love of virtue, and a natural death. Stuck on the lintel above the door there is usually a piece of red paper with two Chinese characters printed on it which mean 'abundant happiness'. Two long red papers are stuck on each side of the door with characters in black or gold bearing appropriate good wishes such as 'May all those entering or leaving through this door find peace'. All these papers are renewed at Chinese New Year and so by the end of the year they are beginning to look weather-beaten and tatty.

The Door Gods

On many doors around the village are pictures of the door gods who have been guarding doors since the Tang

SYMBOLISM

The Five Main Animal Symbols

1. The **Dragon** represents power and the male or *yang* force. It is the symbol of wisdom and of the imperial power. The azure dragon is associated with the east.

2. The **Phoenix** is a mythical bird that never dies, but only appears in times of peace and prosperity. It represents the female or *yin* force and is the symbol of beauty and creativity. It is associated with the empress. The red phoenix from the Cinnabar (red) mountains is associated with the south. Together the dragon and phoenix form a perfect balance (the *yin* and the *yang*).

3. The **Tortoise** with its immensely strong shell is characterized by stability and security, particularly freedom from attack from the north or rear. It symbolizes longevity and is associated with the north.

4. The **Unicorn** is the fourth of the great mythical animals and first appeared to Fu Xi bearing the mythical map from which Chinese calligraphy is said to have evolved. Its characteristics are gentleness and benevolence. In any big celebration in Hong Kong the unicorn dances together with the dragon and lion.

5. The **Tiger**, evoking strength and violence, can both defend and attack. It is the king of the beasts and symbolizes courage and fierceness which are essential for survival but must be carefully controlled. The character for king (王) can be seen on his forehead. The White Tiger is associated with the west.

19

Other Symbols

Bamboo	longevity, endurance (commonly known as the 'Friend of China')
Bat	good luck, joy, and longevity
Butterfly	conjugal happiness
Carp	persistence, success in examinations, martial prowess
Cloud Patterns	blessings, happiness
Crane	longevity. wisdom
Chrysanthemum	autumn, joviality
Deer	longevity
Elephant	wisdom, prudence, and strength
Fish	money (sounds similar to *yu* meaning 'abundance'), success, a wish come true
Gourd	fertility, continuation of the family (contains the elixir of life)
Horse	speed and perseverance
Jade	purity, excellence
Lion	valour, energy, and repeller of evil
Lotus	summer, purity, and perfection
Mandarin duck	conjugal happiness and fidelity
Peach	spring, immortality
Pearl	femininity, beauty, and purity
Peony	spring, love, beauty, and affection
Plum	winter, endurance, and purity
Pomegranate	fertility
Rooster	Protection against evil, success
Unicorn	wisdom
Water	source of breath, wealth
Willow	spring, gentleness, meekness

*Door Gods, Tang Chung Ling
ancestral hall, Fanling*

dynasty (AD 618–907). Emperor Tai Tsung is said to have fallen ill and knew from his dreams that his life was being threatened by evil spirits who invaded his bedroom night after night, keeping him awake all night from fear. The lack of sleep caused him to fall ill. Two of his generals, General Zhou, guardian of the East, and the red-faced General Zhu, volunteered to sit with him in full battle gear, and one of them is reputed to have said, 'Your servant has during his whole life killed men as he would split open a gourd and piled up carcasses as he would pile up ants. Why then should he be afraid of ghosts?'

The generals' vigil was effective, and the emperor slept and began to recover. However, soon after the two generals started to suffer from lack of sleep, so finally the emperor ordered his court painter to paint their likenesses so exactly that the evil spirits would be deceived into thinking they were actually there. The resulting paintings were so successful in keeping the spirits at bay that the generals' pictures have adorned and guarded all manner of houses, temples, and halls ever since.

The *Baat Gwa* Symbol

Above the door is another protective sign against evil spirits and bad luck, the *Baat Gwa* symbol—eight trigrams made up of a combination of triple lines which represent the interaction of the opposing forces of *yin* and *yang*

21

(male and female, hot and cold, north and south). In the centre of the *Baat Gwa*, or sometimes seen on its own, is a circular mirror fixed above the doorway. Its purpose is also to deter evil spirits, working on the premise that they are so ugly that the sight of their own image in the mirror will frighten them away from the door.

The number of these defences shows the importance of the doorway to the house, which leads into the heart of the family and through which all outside influences, both good and bad, enter the house.

The Interior

In the older houses there is often a small courtyard in front of the main rooms. This allows light and air to enter into the home and is known as heaven's well (*tin jeng*). It is here that offerings are made to the gods. The middle room, often seen through an open doorway, is the most important room in the house. It belongs to the entire family and houses the family shrine to its ancestors, which has a red light glowing and offerings of tea or oranges laid in front of it. The sleeping area to the left of the common room is traditionally the parents' room, with the children's sleeping area on the right-hand side of the house. The smaller Hakka village houses partition off the end of the main room to use as a small bedroom, and also use the cockloft above for sleeping purposes.

As you enter a house, immediately to your right is the kitchen with a brick fireplace and shrine to the Kitchen God. Above the small furnace you will see a round hole designed to take the large round wok (cooking pan). The furnace was fed with grass cut from the mountainside or with twigs and sticks. Grass-cutting and the collection of wood was women's work, and if they could collect extra, they would sell it in the market or to the boat people who used it to burn the barnacles off their boats. In this way women could earn a very small private income.

To the left of the entrance, tucked in behind the front door was the family bathing area. A raised stone was set into the floor to stand on, and a large ceramic pot would be filled with water which was scooped out and poured over oneself. In one corner of the main room was a stand with a basin of water on it for washing one's hands and towels hanging from the top. Every morning this was replaced with clean water.

CHAPTER 4

INDUSTRY

Incense

One important industry in the history of Hong Kong is the making of incense sticks, used to honour the gods or family ancestors. These are commonly known as joss sticks, 'joss' being a corruption of *deos*, the Portuguese word for God. The incense was made from the aromatic wood taken from chippings of the *heung*, or, in English, the sandalwood tree (*aquaria sinensis*). By around 1900 Tsuen Wan had twenty-four large mills in which the chippings of the *heung* tree were ground into powder with large hammers powered by water wheels. This powder was mixed with glue and sawdust, and then used to coat bamboo sticks, layer by layer until the incense stick was completed. But even earlier, before 1662, the trade in sandalwood for making incense is thought by some to have given Hong

Kong its name, 'Fragrant Harbour'. It is said that *heung*, meaning 'fragrant', refers not to the sweet-smelling harbour but to the trade in sweet-smelling sandalwood. Wood from the groves of locally grown sandalwood trees was at that time exported to China for processing. This trade came to an untimely end in 1661 during the Great Clearance (see page 4). The population was forced to move inland and the

Incense holder, Yi Tai study hall, Kam Tin   *Incense holder, Kun Ting study hall, Ping Shan*

coastal areas were completely razed. All the *heung* trees were cut down and their stumps burnt. The export of *heung* wood never recovered.

Salt

Salt was produced at a number of sites around the territory. The Imperial Government had a monopoly over salt production and a local salt commission was established as long ago as 100 BC. In Joss House Bay, just behind the Tin Hau temple there, is an inscription dating from the Southern Song dynasty (AD 1274) recording a visit by an officer in charge of the salt administration. The sub-commission for Lantau, established in the tenth century, was so harsh that the Yao people were in an almost continual state of revolt. In 1137, 12,000 troops were sent to wipe out the troublemakers. Lantau did not recover from the devastation for many years until it was finally recolonized by new incomers. In the small Lantau fishing village of Tai O, you can still see the salt pans which were in use as recently as 1937, when they produced as much as 1,488 tons of salt. The seventy acres of former salt pans are still largely intact and undisturbed.

Oysters

Tai Po was the centre of the local pearl industry. As far as we know, pearls were first collected from the nearby sea

Houses overlooking former salt pans, Tai O

Oyster beds, Lau Fau Shan

fishing moved eastwards across to Lau Fau Shan, where oyster beds are tended to this day in family plots, and harvested continually throughout the year, although the oysters are bred for consumption rather than for their pearls. The age-old oyster fisheries, however, are now under threat due to the growing pollution from Deep Bay.

in AD 761 during the fourth year of the reign of the Tang emperor, Hoi Yuen. He established a monopoly on the pearl industry, and, in AD 964, 8,000 soldiers were sent to Tai Po to protect it. The pearls and tortoise shells collected were highly prized and used to adorn an imperial palace in Canton, later burned to the ground.

But the gathering of oysters from the sea bed was no light undertaking. The pearl fisher was tied to a weighted rope, lowered into the sea from a boat, and left in the depths until the boatmen hauled him up with his bag of oysters. If the boatmen were distracted, the pearl fisher would drown. The industry cost so many lives that at least two petitions were filed against this practice. It was stopped in AD 971, only to started again in 1280. The imperial monopoly was finally abolished in 1324.

The decline of the pearl industry was finally ensured when overfishing led to a serious drop in stocks. Oyster

Stone Quarrying and Pottery

Stone is the only commodity in which Hong Kong is still self-sufficient, and quarrying has always been a major industry. The granite extracted from the quarries in East Kowloon, Stonecutter's Island, and Quarry Bay were used throughout the territory and shipped to Canton for building purposes.

Another local industry was pottery-making. The best-known pottery kilns were at the villages of Sheung Wun Yiu, Ha Wun Yiu, and Cheung Uk Tei, south-east of Tai Po Market. China clay and china stone was dug from pits behind Cheung Uk Tei village. An archeological survey of 1995 indicated the scale of the industry as kilns, watermills, a paste-making workshop, and washing basins were excavated. The sites of sixteen watermills were found, each equipped with three to six

Dragon Kilns

sets of pestles and mortars to pound the china clay to the right consistency. Six dragon kilns were located and two excavated. These kilns measured twenty-five metres in length and could accommodate over 10,000 pieces at each firing. The kilns, thought to date back to the mid-fifteenth century, were in continuous production up to the 1930s. The potteries produced large quantities of blue and white rice bowls, remnants of which can still be seen all over the hillside above Sheung Wun Yiu (see page 134). Incense burners, oil lamps and lamp stands, candle holders, ewers, cups, pipes for smoking, and abacus beads were also made. *Kendi* water vessels, used by Muslims for ablutions before visiting the mosque, were produced here too, indicating that pottery was exported over a large area. Shards thought to have originated here have been found as far away as Tioman Island off the east coast of the Malay Peninsula.

CHAPTER 5

HEALTH

The Health of the Local People

At the turn of the century the health of the local population was poor. According to the Maryknoll Mission letters from South China, 50 per cent of the women and children suffered from tuberculosis. Contaminated well water was a major cause of infant mortality (approximately one in five) until midwives were instructed to put disinfectant into village wells. Furthermore, epidemics of cholera regularly swept the territory, and in 1894 there was a fearsome outbreak of bubonic plague which at its height was killing over a hundred people per day. Certain gods are still thanked in annual festivals for delivering the people in that area from these dreaded diseases, such as the god Tam Kung in Shau Kei Wan. Smallpox, malaria, and leprosy were ever-present dangers, and the last leper colony in Hong Kong only closed in the late 1970s; one still exists in Macau.

Coping with Illness

When illness struck, families put off consulting doctors until all else failed because the charges and prescriptions were so expensive that they could easily run into debt. Every village had its wise old women who were knowledgeable in local herb lore and dealt with minor complaints and childhood illnesses. They passed on their knowledge to the next generation.

If an illness proved resistant to home remedies, the family called in the herbalist from the local market town. The herbalists learned their skills by committing to memory an abundance of mnemonic poems. Each poem contained the diagnosis of a particular illness, the ingredients for the relevant prescription, and the expected outcome of the disease. Many of the ingredients could be found locally. Over four hundred medicinal plants growing in Hong Kong are listed in the seven-volume *Chinese Medicinal Herbs* edited by Dr Cheung Siu-cheong. The ingredients for prescriptions were usually dried, ground, or crushed, and taken in the form of soups or teas. In the summer, if you got too much sun from working in the paddy fields, you could drink an infusion of the pineapple-like fruits of the screw pine (*pandanus tectorius*). If your liver or spleen were troubling you, a soup made from the leaves of the spiny bear's breech (*acanthus ilicifolius*) would bring relief. Breathing problems, such as bronchitis, were treated with the flowers of the night blooming cereus. The peeled nut of the longan tree was ground to a powder and used to stop bleeding.

Many of these medicinal plants can be seen carefully labelled with their names and uses in the Medicinal Plants' section at the Lions Nature Education Centre in Sai Kung. Old-style medicine shops and a display of locally used Chinese medicines can be seen in the Museums of History and Medical Sciences (see Appendix).

Closely guarded knowledge of healing herbs and roots found in the wild was passed down in families through the generations. Hok Tsui village on Cape D'Aguilar had (or perhaps still has)

several families who possess these medicinal secrets. The only proviso to this secrecy was that the village headman had to make sure that all villagers could recognize edible herbs from poisonous ones, especially in times of famine.

Age-old folk wisdom concerning the properties of different food and the healing and restorative capacity of herbs, roots, and teas helped regulate daily health in Hong Kong. In the villages in the New Territories, the sun in the heat of the summer could be counteracted with cooling jellies. White jelly was made from the berries of the creeping fig (*ficus pumila*) and black jelly used the juice of the Chinese mesona (*mesona cheninsi*), while cooling soups were made from barley and winter melon. At the approach of the cool winter weather you built up your defences against the cold with 'hearty' soups made of snake or dog meat. The typical Hong Kong mother was busy all day long preparing slow-cooking strength-giving soups for her family— often she still is today.

Chinese Medical Clinics

If a visit to a Chinese medical clinic was necessary, the doctor first observed the tongue, eyes, complexion, pulse, energy level, and symptoms of the patient in order to make his diagnosis.

Medicine shop, Tai Po Market

antlers. Eu Yan Sang at 109–115 Queen's Road, Central, boasts an amazing display of medicines and ingredients, divided into animal, vegetable, and mineral components. In Chinese culture there is no dividing line between food and medicine, and many medicine shops will also display a variety of dried ingredients used to make health-giving soups and dishes.

Teas and Other Health-giving Drinks

Tea is indispensable to the Chinese, both as a drink and as an offering to the ancestors and gods. The mystique of growing, making, and drinking tea has a very long history in China. The habit of drinking tea began as early as the Zhou dynasty (1027–256 BC), while the oldest known essay on tea drinking was written by Wang Bao and Tong Yue in the Han dynasty during the third century BC. Tea drinking seems to have been refined into a ceremony during the Tang dynasty and, to this day, one of the most significant rituals in any wedding is the tea ceremony. The bride and groom, kneeling and bowing low, offer tea, first to their parents, and then to all their close relations in due order, and, in exchange, as a token of acceptance into the family, they are presented with gold jewellery or red (an auspicious colour) packets containing money.

He could then work towards restoring harmony to the body by prescribing particular herbal cures and foods, and banning other foods. If one of the symptoms was a fever, the heat would be counteracted with 'cooling' foods and teas, while 'heating' foods like meat were forbidden.

Medicine Shops

Chinese-style clinics and medicine shops can be found in every town and marketplace in Hong Kong, the latter stocked with innumerable kinds of plants and animal parts, ranging from dried sea horses to deer penises and

Tea is drunk throughout every meal in Chinese restaurants. This is because it is cooling and it counteracts the oiliness of the food. Tea used to grow in both cultivated and wild varieties all over Hong Kong. On Lantau, the bright red *tong fuk* tea was picked from the tea begonia plants which grew on the slopes of Fung Wong mountain, and, until very recently, it was sold at the gates of the Po Lin Monastery there. *Tong fuk* tea is said to have cooling properties, and to relieve sore throats and bronchial problems. Tai Mo Shan, the territory's highest mountain, was famous for a type of green tea which grew wild high up on the mountain side, and was called 'mist' or 'cloud' tea. As recently as 1984, tea was still cultivated for their own consumption on the upper reaches of Kowloon Peak by the Hakka villagers of Mau Tso Ngam.

Tea shop with samovars, Kowloon

Recent studies have shown that green tea, when regularly drunk, can lower a person's cholesterol level by up to 15 per cent and reduce the risk of developing stomach and throat cancer by as much as 50 per cent (as the Cancer Institute and Shanghai Cancer Institute Joint Study reported in the *Hongkong Standard,* July 1996). You can learn more about the history of tea in Hong Kong at the Tea Museum in Hong Kong Park (see Appendix).

To counteract the heat and stress of living in Hong Kong, shops with large brass or copper samovars, decorated with tortoises for longevity, sell medicinal-tasting, health-giving drinks that are very popular among the local people.

CHAPTER 6

EDUCATION

Primary Schooling

In Hong Kong and the New Territories, as in the rest of China, there has always been a profound reverence for learning, with almost every village, at the turn of the century, making some sort of provision for the education of its sons, often in the village temple or ancestral hall. Some villages built primary schools, usually in or near the temple compound. Such schools can be seen at Wun Yu Tsuen, the centre of the pottery industry, and at Tsung Pak Long near Sheung Shui.

Most children had the opportunity to attend school for an average of three years, usually achieving a limited level of literacy. In Sheung Shui it is estimated that approximately 75 per cent of boys between the ages of seven and fourteen received school education. The cost of education was cheap: at the turn of the century families paid between HK$3 and HK$6 per child per annum, with poorer families paying lower fees. Accommodation for students attending the school was provided free of charge by the village, and each child, at the start of his education, brought his own desk and stool. There was no division into classes or year groups, and one teacher taught the whole school. He would divide the school into three groups: one would practice calligraphy; one would recite passages set by the teacher or repeat the new lesson after the teacher; while in the third group the pupils would learn their lessons out loud, to be recited later. Schools were noisy places, echoing with the continual hum of rote learning.

The teacher, who was himself probably an impoverished student, would have been studying for exams, living on a pittance supplemented by measures of rice and gifts from his pupils at festival times. It was likely that he used the four popular textbooks in continuous use since the Song dynasty. From these the children were supposed to learn the basic two thousand Chinese characters. The *Pai Chia Hsing* was the dullest of these four books, consisting entirely of the four hundred most common clan names in China. This clearly demonstrates the importance given to being able to recognize and write family names. The other important task of the teacher was to impart to the young minds of the students the Confucian values of loyalty, filial piety, and righteousness, that were so highly valued by society and by the state.

Education was not easy for the children. Both discipline and learning were reinforced by the liberal use of the cane. Since the written classical Chinese textbooks they used bore no resemblance to the Cantonese or Hakka dialect they spoke at home, they were incomprehensible to them: their

Carp in the study of Tai Fu Tai, San Tin

learning made no sense and the teacher rarely stopped to give explanations. It was usually only after two years of hard work that students began to make sense of their lessons. No wonder, then, that the Chinese symbol for learning is the poor carp struggling to make his way upstream against the swift-flowing currents. This is why the carp is represented in one form or another in many study halls in Hong Kong.

But in understanding Chinese culture, the essential importance of literacy cannot be overlooked. So highly revered was the written word that people were paid to go around and collect up any pieces of paper with writing on them so that they could be respectfully burnt, rather than trodden under foot. Literacy was the cement that bound a vast country speaking many different languages and dialects into a unified whole, as well as providing the key to any sort of advancement. Although the old classical language has been superseded, old attitudes to learning die hard. Chinese parents still expect education to be tough, with an emphasis on long hours and learning by heart; they see no point in allowing the child to 'waste his time' playing.

Study Halls and the Imperial Civil Service Examination

On finishing his primary education, if a student showed promise and was able and willing to continue with his

Kan Yung Shu Uk study hall, Sheung Wo Hang

Perhaps the best example is the recently renovated Kun Ting study hall at Hang Mei Tsuen on the Ping Shan Heritage Trail (see page 89).

It is usual for the study halls to consist of two halls with a light well between the two. At each corner of the main hall are four bays where the students sat at their desks on narrow wooden benches. The upper floors of the bays, reached by a sturdy ladder, served as dormitories for those students living too far away to return home to sleep. One bay was reserved as living quarters for the tutor. He had his desk in the central hall where he could oversee his students' work. At the far end of the main hall there is often an altar dedicated either to the founder or to Man Cheong, the God of Literature.

As you stand in a study hall you can imagine the generations of students, with their brushes and ink, bending earnestly over their calligraphy and composition, or engaged in committing endless pages of the *Confucian Classics* to memory. In this type of study hall there were no classes and no age limits. Each student was a class to himself, working on his own, at his own pace, on tasks set by the teacher. A grandfather might present himself to sit for the Imperial Examination alongside his grandson. If the grandfather reached his eightieth birthday, and had still failed the examination, he might be allowed an honorary pass at the discretion of the emperor, in recognition of his diligence and perseverance.

education, he would transfer to a study hall. These were set up to allow local candidates to prepare for the old Civil Service Examination which dates back to before the Sui dynasty (AD 581–618).

A total of forty-nine study halls have been identified in Hong Kong. Like clan halls, they were mostly prestige buildings which showed the power and political ambitions of the clan. As might be expected, the more imposing and highly decorated halls are owned by the five great clans of the valleys in the New Territories, in particular the powerful Tang clan.

What was it that drove men to study their entire lives away in order to gain a pass at one of the five levels of this formidable examination? There is no real modern equivalent to the sense of honour, reverence, and achievement acquired by securing a pass at any level in this exam. It elevated the social status of the recipient, and brought honour and respect to his entire village. In front of the clan halls, scholar stones can still be seen, celebrating the successful candidates. Flagstaffs used to be attached, but they have long since been removed. Outside the two main clan halls at Hang Mei Tsuen, every passerby, especially those whose surname was not Tang, had to bow before these banners so that no tenant forgot the high status of the Tangs.

Those that achieved a degree (*juren*) were shown great respect throughout their lives and beyond. The graduate was entitled to wear a special gilt button on his hat, and his academic achievements were recorded on his ancestral tablet in the clan hall. A pass at even the lowest level protected a man from corporal punishment, and his family was exempted from taxes, kowtowing, and forced labour (*corvee*). Apart from tutoring, the graduate wrote letters for illiterate neighbours, arbitrated in local disputes, chose names for babies, and was called on to write couplets to hang on each side of the doors during Chinese New Year.

A pass at the second level allowed the recipient to erect a board over his doorway with the date of his pass and the Chinese characters which translate as 'promoted man'. Besides honour and glory, passes at higher levels gave a man with ambition a long and honourable career in the Chinese Civil Service, beginning with an appointment as a District Magistrate. All those passing the highest degree had their names inscribed on scholar stones in Confucius' temple in Beijing. These stones, which can still be seen today with thousands of names carved into them, date back to the thirteenth century.

The first documented Hong Kong man to be awarded a degree was Tang Yim Lun from Lung Yeuk Tau in 1258. The successful local candidates from the Hong Kong study halls brought great prestige to their villages as well as the chance of having a say in local affairs. For this reason rich clan

Scholar stones, Hang Mei Tsuen

Tsang Tai Uk, Sha Tin

Houses, Tai O

Hakka women gathering shellfish on the beach near Fung Hang, Starling Inlet

Tai Fu Tai, San Tin

Village houses, Ha Tin Liu Ha

Town house, Cheung Chau

Pun Uk (Lion House). Hakka house with rice-drying area in front

Sam Tung Uk Hakka village, Tsuen Wan

Sheung Yiu Folk Museum, Sai Kung

Sai Wai, Fanling

Fan Ling Wai, Fanling

Baat Gwa *symbol from a house in Hok Tau Tsuen*

Decorated eaves, Yau Yuen Chang's house, Hoi Pa Gardens, Tsuen Wan

Decorated door panel Tsung Pak Long

Door panel and swallow's tail roof, San Wai. The four papers are the remains of the five blessings.

So Lau Yuen study hall, Kam Tin

Carved folding doors to a study room,
Kun Ting study hall, Ping Shan

Kan Yung Shu Uk, Sheung Wo Hang

Tang Chung Ling clan hall, Lung Yeuk Tau

Liu Man Shek Tong, Sheung Shui

Elders gathered for the reopening of the I Shing Kung Temple, Wang Chau

Loi Shing Tong, Kam Tin

Door Gods, Loi Shing Tong, Kam Tin

Decorated beams, Hau Kui Shek Tong, Ho Sheung
Heung

Roof ridge, Tai Fu Tai, San Tin

Decorated beams, Hau Kui Shek Tong, Ho Sheung
Heung

Liu Man Shek Tong, Sheung
Shui

Painting of scholars at the Tin Hau Temple, Tap Mun Chau

associations or successful and wealthy village elders built study halls and gave scholarships to local boys who excelled in their studies. The successful and wealthy village elder Tang Heung Chuen built the Kun Ting study hall to commemorate his father Tang Kun Ting.

Exam success often aroused intense jealousy and competitiveness in rival clans. In the late 1860s a certain brilliant villager called Tang Yung Keng was one of only three from the New Territories ever to graduate at the highest level in the exam held at the Summer Palace in Beijing. The story goes that, according to custom, his village took him on a celebratory tour so that all the local villages could congratulate him. When he, perhaps unwisely, was paraded in Fan Ling Wai, the main seat of the rival Pang clan, he was invited to a banquet held in his honour, as custom required. That very night the young man died an agonizing death and it was strongly suspected that his wine had been poisoned at the banquet.

To embark on this scholastic obstacle course was a test of courage and faith since every year about two million men from all parts of China took the first examination, and only 1 or 2 per cent were allowed to pass. A thorough knowledge of the *Confucian Classics* was essential, and a vast amount of information had to be memorized. A fifteen-year-old boy was expected to have committed to memory around 400,000 Chinese characters. The examination tested not only literary knowledge and the ability to quote from the Classics, but also the style of the composition, and the balance and beauty of the calligraphy. The age-old method of rote learning, which for so long was the only way to succeed in the Imperial Examination, may account for the important place it still holds in Hong Kong's present educational ladder.

The examinations tested toughness of body and mind as well as academic skills and it was not unknown for candidates to die or go mad during the course of the examination. At the first level the exam lasted one whole day and night, and for the second part, the candidate had to be ready to submit himself to three sessions, each one lasting nearly three days. Thus candidates would arrive carrying writing instruments as well as baskets of hard-boiled eggs and pork to eat, strengthening drinks, bedding rolls, candles, and charcoal in pots to warm their hands. The examination hall in Guangdong covered sixteen acres and consisted of 8,653 separate cells into which the candidates were locked for the duration of the exam. Each cell was only 176 centimetres (5 foot, 9 inches) high and 112 centimetres (3 foot, 8 inches) wide, with rough slots to hold two planks, one to serve as a bench and the other as a desk.

This exam, which was only abolished in 1904, affected Chinese society for thousands of years and its influence is still felt now in the enormous respect given to scholastic achievement. This is demonstrated by the high level of application of Chinese children today in schools all over the world, and the good results they achieve.

The Imperial Civil Service examination system was introduced into Europe by a Spanish missionary, Gonzales de Mondosa, and a Portuguese missionary, Gaspard da Cruz. The written examinations for recruitment into the Civil Service in France, Germany, and Britain are said to have been modelled on the Chinese system.

CHAPTER 7

THE CLAN SYSTEM

If you ask the names of
people from the same
village, the chances are
that they will all have the same
surname. This is due to the clan
system. It was forbidden for girls to
marry anyone with the same surname,
so brides had to marry into the
household and village of another clan.
The men stayed in their own villages,
married wives from other clans, and
brought them home. This system
makes the New Territories a
genealogist's paradise.

The Liu clan of Sheung Shui, now
numbering more than 3,500 members,
can trace their family back in China to
AD 900. The present generation is the
twenty-second or twenty-third to be
born in the New Territories. The
powerful Tang clan can trace its family
back even further. In the eleventh
century, its founding member was the
Mandarin Tang Hon Fu, who stopped
over in Tsuen Wan on his way by boat

to take up the post of
magistrate in Yeung Chun
county. He himself was the
eighty-sixth generation of the
previous Tang clan, and he and
his son, Tang Fu Hip, became the
founding members of the new Tang
clan in the New Territories. Rambling
through the surrounding hills, Tang
Hon Fu was so impressed by the
beauty of the scenery and the excellent
grave sites available that, after finishing
his tour of duty, he uprooted his entire
family, dug up the bones of his
grandparents, and brought them across
China to lay his roots in his new home
territory. Tang Fu Hip settled in the
Kam Tin area in 1069.

There are five great Punti clans in
the New Territories among whom the
Tang is the strongest. Their success is
said to be due to the excellent *fung shui*
of their villages and to their association
with the Song royal family.

Tang Yuen Leung, a member of the

seventh generation of New Territories Tangs, was garrison commander of a town in the north of Guangxi province at a time when the imperial army was falling back in disarray. During the subsequent evacuation 160 people of the royal Song court, mainly women and children, were drowned or scattered. Streams of refugees passed through the town he commanded and he did what he could to alleviate their sufferings, even taking into his home a lost teenage girl who stayed by his side when he retired to Kam Tin. It was not until then that this girl revealed her true identity: she was a princess from the Song emperor's family. In due course she married Tang Yuen Leung's son, and word of her safety and of Tang's kindness reached the emperor, who rewarded the Tang family with a liberal grant of land. The young couple had four sons who founded the four main branches of the Tang clan and settled at Kam Tin, Ping Shan, Tai Po, and at the cluster of villages near Fanling, known as Leung Yeuk Tau. In these villages now lives the twenty-fifth generation of Tangs.

The aristocratic Tangs were landlords and tax lords and extremely powerful in local affairs. In 1726 a villager complained, 'During the day they wanted chicken, geese, and ducks; at night they wanted pretty women in their beds.' An accusation was made at the same time that the Tangs used a grain measure 80 per cent larger than the designated gauge. When the Tangs heard that the county magistrates were on their way to investigate this matter, they arranged for all their young men to gather in the ancestral halls and study halls and pretend to be studying. The magistrates were duly deceived and, thinking that all the Tangs were scholars and therefore above such petty crimes as cheating their tenants, dismissed all charges against them. Such was the power of scholarship.

The four other important clans also have a long history in the territory. The Hau clan arrived in Ho Sheung Heung in the twelfth century and the Pang settled in Fanling soon afterwards. The last to arrive was the mighty Man clan who came from Sichuan province in 1367 and made their base in San Tin. They claim descent from a minister and an army general who took part in the final struggle against the Manchu.

This clan system fosters a high level of responsibility. Every lineage, village, and district produces its own leaders

Inside the Hau Kui Shek Tong, Ho Sheung Heung

The Dajiao *festival, Nga Tsin Wai, Kowloon*

chosen from among its village elders for their achievements and wisdom. These elders represent the interests of their people on the rural consultative committees and in the *Heung Yee Kuk*, the New Territories' body that represents the interests of the local clans to the government. Co-operation and discipline are instilled from a young age through martial arts training, then later through participating in local teams of dragon, lion, or unicorn dancers.

The clan system also gives villagers a strong feeling of unity and belonging. Villagers take great pride in their shared surname, and the composition, ancestry, and family standing of every household is known to them. Great

shame is attached to those who bring the family and clan name into disrepute, so much so that it is very rare for a local to commit a crime in his own village. The village is the nucleus in which villagers are born, moulded, and cocooned, and most of those who leave would choose, if they could, to return to die and be buried there.

This feeling of belonging is strengthened by the great community festival, the *Dajiao*. This takes place regularly in many districts, usually every ten years, with the exception of Cheung Chau which holds its Bun Festival every year. It is organized by a village or cluster of villages to cleanse the area of any ill-disposed and dangerous evil spirits and 'hungry ghosts' (see page 54), and to renew the community's ties with the gods so that peace and harmony may be restored. During this period, no meat is eaten. The local deities, whether temple gods, earth gods, tree or well spirits, are invited to attend and are worshipped by all the villagers at the specially built *Dajiao* altar. The spirits are thanked for watching over the village and are asked to continue to do so. They are then treated to an opera or a puppet show. A huge and dramatic effigy of Yim Lo Wong, the king of Hell, is constructed on a bamboo frame with coloured paper and a papier-mâché head. He is accompanied by Poon Goon, 'the judge', who carries a pencil and notebook to mark down the names of potential troublemakers among the ghosts. Yim Lo Wong then swallows all

Yim Lo Wong with Poon Goon on his right   *Burning of Yim Lo Wong*

the hungry ghosts in the vicinity (hence his enormous belly) before he himself is sent back to hell in a flaming finale on the last night. A recent *Dajiao* ceremony held by the Tang clan, lasting a week, was attended by Tangs from all over the world and cost over HK$3 million.

For a long time the poorer clans have supplemented their incomes through working abroad. One third of all households in San Tin had one or more family member working at sea between 1900 and 1948. Some jumped ship and settled in the United Kingdom, and many more followed suit after World War II. An estimated twenty Man clan millionaires are now settled there. Almost everyone in the New Territories has relatives who have emigrated and are boosting the family fortunes. In Hok Tau, I met a man on holiday from Britain who had left to work in a Chinese restaurant. His three children all have university educations and his daughter had joined the merchant bank, Barings. The family has moved in three generations from rice farming to merchant banking.

Clan Halls

The outward manifestation of the pride, strength, and economic power of a clan is their clan hall. Once you have compared a great ancestral hall in the New Territories with the small local temple, you will see that the heart of Chinese culture lies under its soaring rafters.

40

The earliest of the existing halls dates back to the late seventeenth century. It is likely that older halls were destroyed during the Great Clearance of 1661 (see page 4).

Architecture—Exterior

The largest clan halls consist of three halls separated by two courtyards enclosed with walls. They are usually built from grey bricks and white mortar made with locally produced lime. The entrance hall has a neat symmetry. Its great doors are in the centre and set into the alcove on each side is a raised rostrum. These are known as drum platforms and were used for the village elders to make announcements or for musicians to play on during festivities.

The roof ridges of the hall are often decorated with Shekwan pottery figures, often a pair of dragon fish. These are sturgeon who succeeded in making the ascent of the Yellow River and overleaping the fearsome rapids of Lung-men whereupon they were thought to transform into dragons. They are admired for their struggles in overcoming obstacles and symbolize perseverance. In 1995, a 172-kilogram garoupa fish was ceremonially freed after a total of HK$88,000 was raised to rescue it from a Causeway Bay restaurant: the rescuers thought it might be a dragon fish in disguise. The dragon fish also represents literary eminence and passing examinations with distinction.

Above the main doors are delicate hand-painted pictures, often depicting serene mountain scenes with rippling streams or waterfalls. These scenes are painted to remind the viewers that the mountains are the home of the Taoist gods, and it is believed that men can find peace and harmony for their souls in the natural beauty of the mountain scenery.

The Doors

Beyond the main doors, just inside the clan hall, is a free-standing door frame with another pair of doors. They keep out evil spirits and malevolent ghosts who cannot turn corners and therefore cannot walk around the door frame, as humans can. These doors are kept shut except for very important visiting dignitaries. Door gods (see page 18) are usually painted on the inside of the main doors—in many different shapes, sizes, and colours.

The First Courtyard

Inside the first courtyard a feeling of space and tranquillity prevails. This area is filled to capacity when the clan holds a 'basin feast' for a special occasion (see page 4).

41

Inside the first courtyard, Tang Si Chung clan hall, Hang Mei Tsuen

Steps lead from this courtyard to the second hall. The elegant granite pillars that hold up the roofs of all three halls can be seen. Unlike pillars in Europe where several blocks of stone are placed on top of each other to construct the column, these pillars are carved entirely from one solid block. It would take a craftsman with his hammer and cold chisel the best part of a year to produce one pillar out of an immense block of granite. He would then have to cut out grooves for the wooden beams, some of which slot right through the stone pillar. Although the stone would have been brought by ship to the port nearest to the village, transporting the granite blocks to the site, over rough, primitive tracks would have been exhausting work.

The Roof

In Western buildings the rafters are usually hidden behind ceilings or domes, but in a clan hall the rafters and roof beams are made a focus of interest. They may be painted red, which symbolizes happiness, or green symbolizing peace and eternity. The beams that slot into the pillars and support the roof are often delicately carved with scenes from mythology or auspicious animals and plants. You may find guardian lions displaying their courage, or deer—the only animals able to sniff out the sacred mushrooms that brings eternal life, and therefore symbolizing longevity.

The wooden brackets above the pillars with their branching arms support the weight of the roof. They are called *tou kung* and are typical of Chinese architecture. Similarly designed brackets have been found that date back as early as the East Han dynasty tombs (AD 25–220). This design has been used since in the structure of important buildings. Their size and proportions were formulated

Deer with mushroom, a frieze in the I Shing Kung Temple, Wang Chau

42

from a rigid set of rules by the time of the Song dynasty. The *tou kung* in the clan halls in the New Territories are simple when compared with those in the great temples in Beijing which are often intricately carved and painted.

Altars and Soul Tablets

The second courtyard beyond the second hall contains the ancestral altars. The carved altar surrounds are often rich and colourful with delightful scenes depicting myths and legends or elegant flowers and trees symbolic of long life. You will see rows of slats about eight inches tall and often painted green, the colour of eternity. They are inscribed down the centre in gold with details of the deceased and

Carving on the altar of the Tang Si Chung clan hall, Ha Tsuen Shi

are often adorned at the top with small triangular cones made of gold paper that look like miniature wings.

These slats are known as soul tablets and are traditionally made of chestnut wood. In the larger clan halls the tablets are usually arranged on three altars, the middle one bearing the tablets of the founding ancestor and his sons. These principal tablets are always found at the highest level and the centre altar never changes. The second altar on the right is for clan heroes who fell in battle or particularly distinguished clan members who cast reflected glory on the clan. The left-hand altar is for clan members who contributed funds to the repair and upkeep of the hall. The important details are inscribed on the front of the tablet, but, in addition, a wooden slat fits into the top of the tablet, containing a complete mini biography of that particular clan member.

The altar distinguishes between Hakka and Punti clan halls. The Punti altars have a number of tablets, each

Carved altar surrounding soul tablets, Tsang Tai Uk

Soul tablet, Ha Wo Hang Hakka clan hall

dedicated to a particular individual, while the Hakka altars have only one tablet, with the clan name carved on it, honouring the entire clan.

The custom of enshrining an individual by inscribing a tablet in his honour originated in about 350 BC in the Zhou dynasty. The Lord of Tsui was fleeing from the enemy and was about to die of starvation. His faithful retainer, Kai Tsz-chui, saved his life by cutting off part of his own thigh, cooking it, and feeding it to his master. Weak from loss of blood and unable to keep up, Tsz-chui had to be left on the mountainside. The lord was forever grateful to his attendant and, on his return to safety, sent soldiers to rescue him. However, the soldiers inadvertently set light to the dry grass close to where Tsz-chui lay injured and he

failed to survive the flames. Saddened by his death, the lord consecrated Tsz-chui's name on a wooden tablet in the palace and honoured it daily with incense.

The soul tablets are worshipped in the home until the third or even fourth generation, but there is a limit to the number of tablets that can be given proper attention. So at Chinese New Year the most senior household spirit is invited to join the spirits of the ancestors in the clan hall and to have his name added to the clan scrolls with a short biography.

Thus the clan soul tablets and genealogies constitute priceless historical documents, and many ancient myths and tragedies have been recorded on them. One of the Liao lineage rolls unfolds the story of Liao Chung-shan who lived in Sheung Shui during the Ming dynasty. He was captured by pirates and held for ransom, so his faithful wife offered herself as hostage in his place while her husband returned home to raise the ransom money. The pirates agreed and she secretly told her husband to be sure about her well-being before returning with the money, and gave him a silver ring tied with a strand of her hair. After Liao Chung-shan had followed her instructions, he discovered that she had hurled herself from the ship and drowned, thus saving the family fortune. He mourned her death but took comfort in calling up her spirit with the ring and strand of hair she had left him.

Every year, usually during Chinese New Year, a lavish banquet is set before the ancestors' tablets in the clan hall. It will include whole roast suckling pigs, fish, eggs, fresh fruits, cakes, tea, and wine. Five sets of chopsticks and five bowls are provided for their use, five being an important ritual number in Chinese culture.

The ancestors will extract the essence from the food and drink, leaving their descendants to enjoy the real food itself. Thus the ancestors are cared for and are reassured of the prosperity of the clan since it can afford to put on such a feast. Sharing food with their ancestors gives the clan a feeling of closeness and unity.

All ceremonies to honour the ancestors, both in the home and in the ancestral hall, must be performed exclusively by men. In Chinese traditional families women take second place. Until a few years ago they did not even have the right to inherit property which instead was passed either to the woman's sons or to her husband's brothers. In 1994 legislation was introduced that allowed the women of the New Territories to inherit land, but it is still bitterly disputed.

Uses of the Clan Hall

The clan hall is not only a place for the worship of clan ancestors, it also acts as a council chamber for clan elders who are still summoned to meetings by a messenger who walks the length and breadth of the village beating a gong. The elders are powerful figures in the local community. They mediate in all kinds of disputes and solve problems. In the past village elders could pass sentence and inflict corporal punishment in the clan hall. However, if the crime was serious the offender was handed over to the government for trial. The elders would also take charge of local security, organizing a watch system against thieves, bandits, or floods, and arranging for the protection of the village in case of attack.

The elders still have the responsibility for clan finances. Over the years rich and pious clansmen have given land and money to pay for the proper care of their ancestors. These trust funds may run into millions of Hong Kong dollars. In the Man clan hall in Sheung Shui, in one year more than HK$60 million passed through the accounts, which were displayed on the notice board.

The elders have to decide how best to invest the money and on what the income should be spent—widows may be supported, kindergartens organized, or scholarships awarded. Temples and shrines are maintained and the *Dajiao* (see page 39) is celebrated. However when a clan has not prospered and feels that the ancestors have let them down, the clan hall is neglected and may fall into decay. The relationship between the living and the dead is of mutual benefit and both sides must play their role for it to work.

CHAPTER 8

BELIEFS AND TRADITIONS

O ur deepest hopes and fears are expressed in our religious beliefs and customs. Some understanding of Chinese religion, as it is practised in Hong Kong, can tell us much about the fundamental values and attitudes of the Chinese living in the territory. A newcomer to the Chinese culture will see gaudy temples and demonic-looking statues that may seem primitive and pagan, but they actually represent profound and ancient beliefs and traditions that underly the code of behaviour and mindset of the Hong Kong people, and provide a rich source of myth and legend.

Hong Kong is one of the few Chinese places where beliefs and customs have been preserved undisturbed through the ages, from as far back as prehistoric times right up to the present day.

Chinese religious beliefs and attitudes towards religion are very different from those in the West. I have used the word 'beliefs' rather than 'religions' in this case since 'religion', as defined in the *Oxford English Dictionary*, is 'the belief in a super-human controlling power entitled to obedience and worship'. In contrast, the three main Chinese philosophies, Taoism, Confucianism, and Buddhism, have no governing metaphysical being. The Chinese have a freedom, not found in institutional religions such as Christianity or Islam, to incorporate under the umbrella of popular religion a wide, diffuse, and often contradictory web of beliefs, philosophies, and legends. People can integrate their beliefs and religious practises in a way that suits them, usually by following family tradition, and they are free to practise these beliefs when, where, and how they choose. No particular day is set aside for worship as in other religions.

Perhaps it is this lack of organization in Chinese religion that has led to an informal division into two distinct traditions. On the one hand there is the 'high' tradition in which the teachings of Confucianism, Taoism, and Buddhism are kept separate. Each philosophy has its own ancient writings which are studied and interpreted by a few learned and committed sages who teach their disciples to find a deeper meaning in their faith. For the lay person, however, the three beliefs are inextricably combined. This has led to a 'low' or popular tradition, handed down orally through the generations with a more pragmatic and practical approach to religion. It is more closely related to the needs of the people with an emphasis on health, wealth, position in society, and happiness. These two traditions interact at many different levels.

The monks, priests, or sages from the 'great tradition' are drawn from the local community and perform important rites such as house blessings or funerals. Recently when accidents occurred at the newly enlarged Happy Valley race-course, Buddhist monks were brought in to give it a special blessing. After heavy rains in July 1996 caused a landslip at Fanling Cemetery, destroying more than 200 graves, Taoist priests performed rituals to appease the spirits of those who had been disturbed. The best known and most respected sages from the 'great tradition' have been adopted by the people to join the family of gods and are revered in temples.

Chinese religion can be seen as a river of belief flowing and eddying down through the ages. At various times in history different beliefs have emptied their waters into this river while scarcely disturbing the waters flowing down from further back. Thus, unlike in Europe where earlier beliefs and customs, such as druids and witches, were ruthlessly stamped out, the different strands of Chinese belief were all incorporated into Taoism, Confucianism, and Buddhism. These earlier beliefs and traditions are known as 'Shamanism', thought by some to be one of the oldest religions in the world.

Shamanism

By the time of the earliest recorded dynasties of Shang (c. 1600–1027 BC) and Zhou (c. 1027–221 BC) these beliefs had spread from their homeland in Siberia down through China. They also crossed the Bering Straits to Alaska and took a hold among the Red Indian tribes of America. In China, Shamanism became the state cult and the Shamans or priests acted as mediums to bridge the gap between humans and the spirit world by going into trances and seeking answers through oracles or divination. They believed that the earth was a holy place that humans should honour and protect. The earth was thought of as a product of delicately balanced forces with which humans interfere at their peril, and which was inhabited by

Earth God Shrine, Luk Keng

guardian spirits that dwell all around us.

The oldest of the Chinese gods inhabit the stones of the earth, the heart of the trees, and the waters of the wells, and protect the houses and families. The Door Gods and the Kitchen God are given special attention at Chinese New Year (usually in late January or early February, according to the lunar calendar) when they are thanked for past blessings and asked for favours and protection in the coming year. In the Outlying Islands and New Territories you can see shrines to these ancient gods, clean and tidy with new red papers and offerings of tea, incense, and oranges. The most important of these spirits are the Earth Gods, the Tree Gods, and the Kitchen God.

Earth God Shrines

The innumerable Earth God Shrines scattered throughout the territory are proof of the endurance of traditional beliefs and customs. These gods are responsible for the well-being of small local areas, which vary in size from a house to a whole village. The Earth God resides either in a niche set into the back wall of the shrine or in the stone set in the middle of an armchair-shaped altar at the village's entrance. The Earth God or 'To Dei Gung' is also sometimes called 'Fuk Dak Jing San' meaning 'True God of Good Fortune and Virtue'. The name is usually printed on red paper or carved in the stone at the back of the altar. In village clusters like Sheung Shui or Kam Tin, each hamlet has its own altar. You will also see Earth God Shrines at every temple or monastery you visit.

Each Earth God is part of a hierarchy of Earth Gods ordered according to the size of their territory. He protects the inhabitants and registers births, deaths, and marriages in Heaven. All importatnt local events are reported to him. After a death he will guide the soul safely through the regions of darkness if properly propitiated, thus ensuring a safe journey through the depths of the Underworld. The God is often portrayed as an old man with a crooked staff in one hand and a boat-shaped gold bar in the other. The Earth Gods are themselves ruled by the City God, Sing Wong, and report to him on those under their care.

Tree God Shrine, Ha Wo Hang

Tree Shrines
Particular trees are important as dwelling places for the tree spirits. You may find incense sticks or a small shrine at the base of a special tree. These tree spirits are used as the first line of defence when sickness strikes in a family. Children were (and perhaps still are) entrusted to a tree spirit's care in an adoption ceremony and then released when they reached adulthood. Banyan trees are often chosen for worship as tree gods because their trailing branches and aerial roots give the appearance of multiplicity and therefore fertility.

Kitchen God Shrines
The Kitchen God was, and may still be, the most common god found in the home. His main duty is to report to the Jade Emperor in Heaven on the behaviour of his particular household. A few days before Chinese New Year, his image is burnt to send him on his way, but before he leaves he is fed sweet sticky rice to bribe him into saying good things to the Jade Emperor. His lips may be so sticky with golden syrup that his report will be short. The Kitchen God returns on New Year's Eve for another year's vigil and is welcomed home with a clean shrine and offerings of incense and tea.

Well Shrines
Each village well has a shrine dedicated to the Well God. It is surprising how many wells have survived, although the shrines have mostly disappeared. However, references to the Well God can be found from at least the third century BC.

Sacred Rocks
Special rocks around the territory are revered and some, imbued with the

Well God Shrine, Tap Mun Chau

49

spirit of fertility, are visited by engaged couples or anxious grandmothers hoping for male offspring.

There is one such rock on Hong Kong Island at the eastern end of Bowen Path which runs above and parallel to Kennedy Road. This rock is called Tse Sun Niang-niang which translates as 'She who furnishes Posterity'. It is well patronized and noticeably phallic in shape, and the path up to the rock is bordered by shrines to Buddhist and Taoist gods. It is well worth the climb up to the rock for the spectacular view over Hong Kong and Victoria Harbour.

Ancestor Worship

Since prehistoric days, ancestor worship has bound together the extended family or clan, the most important unit of Chinese society. In China the individual is subservient to the family and strives to keep it united and happy.

The relationships of the clan members living and dead, can be compared with a great banyan tree. The roots are the souls of deceased family members now in the Under-world and unseen. They strive to provide nourishment and stability for the rest of the tree which represents the living family. The leaves symbolize the mature family members who are working to ensure the family's present prosperity, and nurturing the next generation. The tree trunk depicts the body of clan elders who provide the wisdom and experience of their age and from the generations that have since past on. Clan elders perform the rites whereby offerings are presented to the souls in the Underworld. Ancestors then reciprocate with blessings and favours that, in turn, will ensure the good health of the family and clan. This role gives a special status and importance to the elderly. In the family, as in the tree, all parts are interdependent and equally important to the health of the whole.

To ensure that the deceased clan members rest in peace and help continue the clan's prosperity, they must be buried according to tradition and have their needs satisfied in the afterlife.

Almost life-size paper car

50

As far back as the Shang dynasty the dead were buried in great tombs containing all they needed in the afterlife. In these tombs archaeologists have found remains of people who appear to have been buried alive without any signs of struggle, including courtiers, concubines, attendants, and charioteers, together with their chariots and horses. The tomb of Fu Hao, one of the many consorts of King Wu Ding who died and was buried in about 1200 BC, was found to contain sixteen human skeletons to serve her in the afterlife, as well as 1.5 tonnes of bronze shaped into hundreds of tools and useful objects. There was also a profusion of jade, stone, bone, and ivory items, including several hundred hairpins.

Over the years, the ritual of sacrificing humans and animals ceased, and clay figurines were substituted for the attendants and animals, as well as for large bulky objects such as houses and chariots. If you walk down Hollywood Road in Central, you will see the antique shops overflowing with these replicas.

But nowadays more practical and cheaper paper likenesses which, unlike pottery, do not take up valuable space are used instead of pottery. In this way the departed are still furnished with all they might need in the afterlife. During the funeral, goods are sent up to them by being burnt as offerings. Today, a five-foot paper model of a two-storey house, fully furnished and including a Filipino maid and Sikh doorman costs

HK$700, while a life-size model of a Mercedes Benz is HK$500. Even mobile phones, credit cards, and chequebooks are included in the offerings these days. Piles of replica money, found on the shelves of the Wellcome Supermarket, are burnt for deceased loved ones to spend in the afterlife. Shops making and selling paper replicas for burial rites or for worship of the gods can be found all over the territory.

Burial Customs

When you walk in the wilder parts of the New Territories or Outlying Islands, you may notice three types of graves on the hillsides. In the first stage of burial a grave is hastily dug on a hillside to receive the body of the newly deceased, and a plain and roughly inscribed grave stone is erected. This will be the resting place for the body for between five and ten years. This grave is then dug up and the bones are carefully and respectfully removed by a specialist who cleans, purifies, and arranges them in a neat orderly manner inside a large, earthenware funerary urn, usually yellowish-brown in colour. This urn is tightly closed with an inner and outer lid and put on the hillside with other urns. They are known as 'golden pagodas'. A small white hut, like a miniature house, is often built to shelter the urn.

The family visits the urns during one or both of the Chinese public holidays specifically allocated for grave-

Horseshoe-shaped Grave

sweeping in Hong Kong: the Ching Ming Festival in the spring and Chung Yeung in the autumn. At these times the family clears away the undergrowth and coats the urn with lime to prevent the growth of moss and mildew.

The burial process usually finishes at this stage, but in the case of a much-revered family head or a wealthy family it may continue to the third stage. The family, aided by a geomancer, will search for a permanent site where the spirit of the deceased will glean special comfort from its harmony with nature, and therefore be better able to aid the family. The most highly prized sites are found on south-facing hillsides overlooking water. Here a more imposing grave, shaped like a wide horseshoe, will be made, and a formal gravestone erected, giving details of the relationships of the

family members and who have paid for the grave. The family venerates the ancestor with offerings of his favourite food and drink, and burns spirit money for his use in the afterlife. Traditionally, they would also set off firecrackers to scare away any evil spirits, but firecrackers are now illegal so the practice is very rare in Hong Kong. Nowadays only indigenous villagers are allowed this type of grave and then only in the designated village burial area.

Destroying or damaging a grave is taken very seriously. The family and clan of the deceased fear that the spirit, angered by their negligence in failing to care dutifully for the grave, will punish them with sickness or disaster. Recently, a grave threatened with removal to provide space for a land fill, has led to a bitter dispute between the Tang clan in Ping Shan and the Government, and to the closing of the

Ching Shu Hin guest house and the Kun Ting study hall. The clan was offered over HK$2 million in compensation money, but they claim that no amount of money can compensate for the loss of good fortune from disturbing an important ancestor's grave.

Communication with Ancestors

From Neolithic times (c. 3000 BC) Shamans used divination to discover the will of the dead and so enable the rulers to receive blessings and escape punishments and calamities. Diviners heated the carefully prepared shoulder bones of oxen or shells of tortoises and examined the patterns of cracks the heat produced. Some of China's earliest-known writings, dating from the Shang dynasty are in the form of questions posed to ancestors, written on these bones.

Today ancestors are still honoured on family altars in homes and in clan halls all over the territory. A red light is kept constantly burning, while tea and incense are regularly offered, and gifts such as pork, chicken, or oranges on special days.

Ancestral Tablets

When someone dies, his soul is thought to divide itself: part of the soul hangs over the grave and the remaining part takes up residence in the ancestral tablet (see page 43) on the forty-ninth day after the person's death. This occurs during a special ceremony when the Taoist priest or village elder officiating adds in bright red ink the missing stroke to a Chinese character on the inscription. This extra stroke changes the character *wang* (王), meaning 'king', into *chu* (主), meaning 'lord'. The tablet is then passed to the eldest son who places it in its niche on the family shrine.

After the funeral rites, the spirits of the departed are cared for and worshipped in the small family shrines which are situated in the front rooms of village houses. The tea and incense offered daily and the special foods offered on particular occasions give the spirits comfort and a sense of well-being in the Underworld so that they will, in turn, watch over and help the living members of the family. An unworthy action by a family member is an offence against the ancestors, and famine, defeat, sickness, or death are the penalties which the spirits may mete out to those who dare displease them.

The ancestors can only be properly worshipped if there is a male heir. This ensures a position of special importance to sons, particularly the eldest. Mencius (c. 372–289 BC), the most illustrious follower of Confucius, went so far as to say that the greatest crime a son can commit is to fail to provide an heir. In the past, if the first wife could not produce a son, a concubine would be sought. She was often chosen by the first wife and was subordinate to her. In Hong Kong concubinage was only made illegal in

1971, so there are many still alive in the territory.

Hungry Ghosts

A spirit with no family to care for his well-being becomes a 'hungry' or an 'angry' ghost and, unchecked, can expend its anger in unpredictable ways. So dangerous and feared are the angry ghosts that money is always forthcoming for special ceremonies at the time of the *Yue Lan* or the Hungry Ghost Festival in August when the gates of the Underworld open and ghosts roam the Earth. Food, drink, and entertainment are provided and money burnt to appease the wandering ghosts.

Confucianism

> By enquiring into all things, understanding is made complete; with complete understanding, thought is made sincere; when thought is sincere, the mind is as it should be; when the mind is as it should be, the individual is morally cultivated; when the individual is morally cultivated, the family is well regulated; when the family is well regulated, the state is properly governed; and when the state is properly governed, the world is at peace.
>
> From *Daai-hok*, one of the 'Four Books' of Confucian classical literature

This quotation sums up Confucian thought on the essential role of education in producing the 'morally cultivated' individual. Confucius (551–479 BC) was born into an obscure family from the small state of Lu. His father, a military officer, died when he was three years old so he was brought up by his lone, impoverished mother. He worked his way up the Civil Service in Lu until he became Chief Minister and, according to legend, he left the government in disgust after the king was so beguiled by a troupe of dancing girls that he neglected the affairs of state.

Confucius then set out to establish a set of moral precepts that would guide the conduct of the king and his people, and restore peace and order to the state. For inspiration he looked

Confucius, Kan Yung Shu Uk study hall, Sheung Wo Hang

Calligraphy in the Tang Si Chung clan hall, Ha Tsuen Shi, showing the Confucian principles of (left) hau *(filial piety) and* tai *(fraternal love).*

back to the legendary era of Huang Di, the Yellow Emperor (see page 2), building on what he admired from the past, including ancestor veneration. His writings constitute a philosophy rather than a religion, though after his death Confucius was accorded the respect of a god throughout China, with temples dedicated to him in all the larger cities.

Confucius taught that the world was regulated by a natural order that was essentially good. He believed that all relationships, whether between the emperor and his subjects, or husband and wife, or parents and their children, should be natural and harmonious and based on loyalty and cooperation, backed by a strong sense of responsibility for order in society. Man's nature was pure at birth, but could be tainted by ignorance and bad experience. It was the duty, therefore, of everyone to guard their innocence and to educate their children to do the same. Children should be taught a deep sense of filial respect, knowing their

proper place within the hierarchy of the home and of society. The five great virtues that were and still are instilled in children are benevolence, justice, propriety, wisdom, and sincerity. Of these the greatest virtue was *ren* (or *jen*) meaning benevolence combined with a deep concern for others.

The emperor held a mandate from Heaven to rule and could only maintain Heaven's support if he ruled virtuously, aided by his civil servants whose education was thoroughly grounded in Confucian teachings. From these teachings evolved the idea of the scholar-gentleman. The true gentleman should be steeped in learning, particularly the knowledge of the five great classics: the *Book of Changes* (I Ching), the *Book of History*, the *Book of Songs*, the *Classic of Rites*, and the *Spring–Autumn Annals*. His studies would develop a deep ethical commitment to and compassion for others. He would be honest, frugal, and hard working, and always striving to improve society and government.

Chinese students all around the world, whether in Canada, Australia, or the United Kingdom, surprise their teachers with their dedication and conscientiousness, which is the legacy of Confucius. According to a survey carried out recently in Hong Kong by Prudential Assurance and reported in the *South China Morning Post*, 94 per cent of those interviewed believed that children had a responsibility to support their parents financially. Of the working people interviewed, 82 per cent regularly gave money to their parents, regardless of whether their parents were retired. The average amount given was HK$2,575 per month, with low-income earners just as willing to contribute as high-income earners.

Both the Taoists and the Confucians believe in the essential goodness of man, but Confucius was concerned about society in a practical and élitist way, whereas Taoist thinkers concentrate on the individual and the path that leads to fulfilment.

Taoism

Why are *fung shui* experts among the highest-paid people in Hong Kong? Why is all food and drink divided into strict categories according to their 'heating' and 'cooling' capacities? Why are Chinese gardens and pictures inevitably filled with rocks and water? The answers to these and many other questions about Chinese culture lie in the philosophy of Taoism.

> When you gaze at something
> but see—nothing;
> When you listen for a sound
> but cannot hear it;
> When you try to grasp it
> and find it has no substance
> —then these three things
> That go beyond your mind
> Are moulded together in the One.

These lines are taken from the *Tao Te Ching* (Chapter 14, translated by

Laozi on the water buffalo

Palmer, Kwok, and Ramsey) which loosely translates as *The Book of the Way and its Power*. According to tradition, its author, Laozi, was over ninety years old and tired of government work when he decided to retire and leave the province. As he was riding on a water buffalo over a mountain pass, he was stopped by a border guard who begged him to record his wisdom for posterity. Laozi sat down there and then and wrote the book which became one of the great Taoist classics.

Tao defies translation, definition, and understanding because it is beyond the scope of language. In the *Tao Te Ching* it is explained in these lines:

> The Tao that can be talked about is not the
> true Tao.
> The name that can be named is not the
> eternal Name.

It can only be recognized through symbols: the flowing water, the sexual act, the mountains, and the valleys. A master cannot teach anyone else to find the Way. He may point the student in the right direction, but ultimately each

YIN AND YANG

The characters for yin and yang portray the effect of sunlight falling on a hill. One side is bright, the other is in shadow.

Hill	People under a roof	Cloud	*Yin*

Hill	Sun above the horizon	Rays of light	*Yang*

person must find his own Way.

The heart of Taoism is captured in Chapter 42 of the *Tao Te Ching*:

The Tao gave birth to one, the origin.
The one, the origin, gave birth to the two.
The two gave birth to the three.
The three gave birth to every living thing.

'The two' referred to here are *yin* and *yang*, and 'the three' are the triad of Heaven, Earth, and Humanity; the principle of polarity is at the heart of Taoist thought. The rhythmic flow of nature consists of two opposing forces which, by complementing each other, hold the key to life when in balance. *Yin* is negative, female, dark, soft, and passive, whereas *yang* is positive, male, light, hard, and active. Where these two forces achieve perfect harmony and balance, there is Tao. It is the source of all energy, but is itself still, immoveable, and immortal. Nature,

57

THE EIGHT IMMORTALS

Immortal

Symbol

1. Han Zhong Ni (Han dynasty) Alchemist and marshal of the Empire who retired to the Mountains.

Feathered Fan

2. Lu Dong Bin (Tang dynasty) Government official, Patron Saint of literature who retired to the mountains of Shanxi. Associated with healing, he carries a magic sword given to him by the fire dragon.

Fly Whisk to sweep away the clouds

3. Li Tie Guai His body having been cremated by his disciple, he assumed the body of a lame beggar. Fights for the poor and weak. Often accompanied by a deer.

Iron crutch Gourd stocked with magical drugs to relieve pain and disease.

4. Zhong Guo Lao (Tang dynasty) Had supernatural magic powers but preferred the life of a hermit. Rides backwards on a white mule that could be folded up and put away in his cap box.

Bamboo tube and rods

5. Han Xiang Zi (Tang dynasty) Associated with Horticulture. Personifies youth and music

Jade flute

THE EIGHT IMMORTALS

Immortal

Symbol

6 Cao Guo Jiu (Song dynasty)
Represents officialdom. Withdrew to
the mountains where he was adopted
by the Immortals to fill the last vacant
grotto in the upper sphere. Patron Saint
of the Theatre. Depicted in winged
court headdress and official robes.

Castanets

7. Lan Cai He (Tang Dynasty)
Hermaphrodite and eccentric with a
disregard of money. Plays the flute
and represents youth.

Basket of flowers

8. He Xian Gu (Tang Dynasty)
The only female. A Chinese Cinderella
rescued from a life of drudgery by
Han Zhong Ni, she wandered the hills
with her kitchen ladle living on powdered
mother of pearl and moonbeams.
Later transformed into a lotus.

Lotus

with its constant cycle of change, birth,
and decay, is the pathway that can lead
man to Tao.

The aim of Taoism in life and art is
the harmony which flows from a
proper balance of *yin* and *yang*. Taoists
see the constantly changing cycles of
nature in our world as the earthly signs
of a great and universal force, referred
to above as 'the origin'. This force, from
which all being comes, is likened to a
void, an emptiness of 'non-being' (the
biggest temple on Cheung Chau is
called the 'Temple of Jade Vacuity' for
this reason). Fulfilment is found in
fusing the individual's life with the ebb
and flow of nature, whose life force,
otherwise known as *qi*, comes from
being in harmony with the void at the
centre of the cosmos. In *Taoist Song*, Ji
Kang (AD 223–262) explains it in the
following passage:

Frieze outside the Ha Wo Hang clan hall

I will cast out Wisdom and reject
  learning;
My thoughts shall wander in the silent
  Void
I cast my hook into a single stream
But my joy is as though I possessed a
  Kingdom.

Complete harmony with Tao leads to immortality, as was achieved by the 'Eight Immortals' who made their homes in the 'Sacred Mountains of China'. Travelling throughout the land, they used their gifts to help good, hard-working folk labouring under oppression and hardship, and their stories are well known. The search for immortality has given Chinese people a deep regard for longevity since, in old age, a person may have the experience and the freedom from distraction that will bring him nearer to his Tao.

Those seeking to follow the Tao turn to nature and, in particular, to the remote and silent mountains where, undisturbed by worldly worries related to society, work, and competition, they can meditate and learn to act spont-

aneously in accordance with the rhythms of nature, and make progress along the Way.

Thus the mountains of China have a special significance in Taoism, because they are home to the gods and the immortals, and because there man can become close to nature. This is why so many temples depict mountain scenery, often showing sages meditating among the rocks or imparting their wisdom to their disciples.

Taoism was almost wiped out in China by the Cultural Revolution (1966–75) but is now staging something of a comeback. In 1985 there were only 2,500 ordained monks left in the whole of China. By 1995 there were 12,000 with growing links to the Taoist movement abroad. In 1996 for the first time ever, seven Taoist monks from China attended a religious conference in England.

In the following sections I have tried to show how Taoist ideas have entered into many facets of life and, to this day, influence how Hong Kong

60

people think and act on a number of subjects.

Taoism and the Healing Arts

Over the centuries, seekers of the Way journeyed to the mountains to meditate and seek immortality. In their quest for the miracle of immortality, they tried out thousands of herbs, seeds, roots, flowers, insects, and animal parts which they brewed and drank, by chance discovering the many healing properties of their concoctions. Hermits and Shamans used this knowledge to cure people, selling herbs in the temples to support their needs. In this way medicine became linked to religion and the larger temples such as Wong Tai Sin, or the Taoist monasteries such as Ching Chung Koon in Tuen Mun, still have medical halls attached where Chinese medicine is dispensed free of charge to the needy.

Taoism regards man as a triangle of three elements, the body, the mind, and the spirit. To reach harmony, or Tao, and achieve immortality, man must unite these three elements. This is fundamentally different from Christianity where at death only the spirit goes on into the next world leaving the now useless body behind. But in Taoism the body cannot be separated from the soul: both are necessary in the afterlife. This is why traditional Chinese dread losing a body part in surgery and are very reluctant to donate body organs to medical science. Taoists therefore place great importance on the well-being of the body. A Taoist master may not be able to teach someone how to reach his personal Tao, but he can advise him on how to maintain his body through a healthy diet and regular exercise to achieve the necessary balance and harmony to journey along the Way. During illness an imbalance is created which destroys the harmony, but the Taoist masters help to restore this.

To this day many Chinese prefer this more holistic approach to medicine which treats the body, mind, and spirit as equally important in the trinity that makes up the individual's complete being. It is reported that up to a thousand people visit the free herbalist clinics at the Tung Wah group of hospitals every day. A Chinese proverb says,

Screw pine, used to treat sunstroke

61

'You do not start to dig a well when you are thirsty'. Likewise the Chinese believe that maintaining good health should be continual, not instigated only when there is illness. In previous ages the wealthy would keep a family doctor whose job it was to ensure that the family stayed healthy, and any illness among family members was considered a failure on his part.

Unlike Western medicine, Chinese medicine is not designed to cure the ailment immediately. The treament will be spread over time, and the prescription will be revised regularly according to the symptoms. The lifestyle and diet of the patient will also be monitored to prevent the ailment from recurring. Gradually the body will return to its equilibrium and the person's health will be restored. To a Chinese doctor, Western medicine only cures the symptoms, disregarding the underlying imbalances and allowing the unnatural condition to return.

Taoism and the Martial Arts

Taoism regards man's health as being dependent on his vital energy, known in Chinese as *qi*. To strengthen one's *qi* is fundamental to strengthening one's overall health. From early on in history Taoist masters developed practices aimed at helping people to nurture their *qi*, some of which were exercises based on natural movements and used in self-defence. Various schools of martial arts developed from this, including judo, qigong, tai chi chuan, and tae kwan do.

Tai chi chuan consists of slow, balanced movements which activate the *qi* in the body and which are believed to improve the equilibrium of the mind and body, strengthen the internal organs, and improve peace of mind. According to legend, these exercises originated from attempts by early masters to copy and the movements of birds and animals. This is reflected in the names of some of the movements, such as the 'cat looking at the moon', the 'crane standing on one leg', or the 'swallow returning to its nest'. It is a common sight to see people practising their tai chi chuan very early in the morning around Hong Kong.

Taoism and the Fine Arts

Painting and calligraphy were used to give the artist a better understanding of the journey to complete harmony. Since Taoism was a philosophy that could not be easily expressed in words, paintings were used to communicate ideas and truths about nature and the universe.

Paintings, called 'silent poems' by the poet Su Tung Po (AD 1036–1101), were originally created in temples as a devotional exercise to concentrate the mind. The basic aim of the artist was to express his belief in the universal order and his desire for harmony with Tao. For this reason nature was portrayed in all its grandeur and man as insignificant. Painters tried to harness their emotions, free their minds, and train their hands in their paintings so that creative energy—'the breath of

TAO

A single character is usually made up of different elements and therefore, to a reader of Chinese, can convey many shades of meaning. The word Tao is usually translated as 'path' or 'way', but Tao has other meanings too. It can refer to the way of doing things, the path of the universe, or the way of life that Taoists follow.

Furthermore the character for Tao symbolizes an inner way as well as an outward path. The character for Tao is a combination of the two characters that represent the words 'head' and 'foot'. The character for 'foot' suggests the idea of a person setting their feet on a path in a particular direction. The character for 'head' suggests the thinking person's conscious choice. But 'head' also suggests a beginning and 'foot' an ending, both for the person setting his feet on the path and for the universe in its continuing course.

The character for Tao demonstrates the Taoist idea that the eternal Tao is both moving and unmoving. The 'head' in the character represents the beginning the source of all things or the Tao itself which never moves or changes; the 'foot' is the movement on the path.

foot   **head**   **Tao**

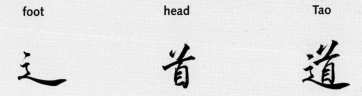

life'—could help them achieve unity with their subject.

By adhering to the principles of *yin* and *yang* the artists harmonized the elements they were depicting. In an attempt to capture the feeling of change and motion in the continual cycle of life, mountains and foothills were balanced by streams and lakes, distant landscapes by close-ups of animals, flowers, or trees, and movement by stillness. The *yang* colours of red, white, and gold had to be balanced by the *yin* colours of blue, green, black, and silver.

In the Xubaizhai Gallery on the second floor of the Museum of Art in Tsim Tsa Tsui you can see some examples of these paintings. This collection dates from the Six Dynasties period (AD 220–581) up to this century.

Calligraphy was practised according to the same principles. In both painting and calligraphy, rhythm, line, and form are blended into a harmonious whole that echoes the balance in the universe. The natural world was considered an important inspiration and calligraphers had to give their characters a sense of movement that reflected *qi*. Every character had to be centred and balanced and controlled, with the spaces between the strokes as important as the strokes themselves. From the fourth century, monks practised calligraphy as part of their religious exercises to help them learn to concentrate and meditate.

As you go round the various clan halls, particularly the Tang clan hall at Ha Tsuen Shi and the Man Mo Temple in Tai Po Market, you will see some beautiful examples of calligraphy, but perhaps the finest are to be found in the new Chinese garden near Kai Tak where the Kowloon Walled City once stood.

Tao and Chinese Gardens

Garden design has an ancient history in China. The earliest known description is in the *Book of Songs* (fifth century BC) in which a poem describes a Chinese garden with its lotus lake, winding streams, and balconied pavilion overlooking the water.

Like paintings, gardens represent an attempt to recreate the beauty, balance,

Garden at the Yuen Yuen Institute

and grandeur of nature in miniature, according to the principles of *yin* and *yang*. Balance and polarity are of utmost importance. Trees and flowers can be better appreciated against a contrasting background of empty white walls and spacious courtyards. Hard, jagged rocks representing *yang* are balanced by softly flowing water. Stones that have been pitted and eroded by water have the true quality of Tao, as they suggest the inter-penetration of *yin* and *yang*. The *Tao Te Ching* puts this beautifully (in Chapter 43) when it says:

> The very softest thing of all
> Can ride like a galloping horse
> Through the hardest things.
> Like water penetrating rock.
> And so the invisible enters in.

There is an old Chinese saying that states that the greater strength lies in

Moon gate, Ching Chung Koon Monastery

colours, reinforcing the idea of change and mutation. Classical poems and elegant names for the different parts of the garden were used to help set the mood for tranquil appreciation and relaxation that would lead to a renewal of *qi*.

There are many gardens and quiet corners throughout the territory that have been designed according to Taoist ideals. In particular, the new garden planted on the site of the old Kowloon Walled City is a very beautiful memento to this historical place. The gardens at Wong Tai Sin Temple and Ching Chung Koon Monastery are also worth visiting; the latter has a magnificent collection of bonsai trees.

the weak: 'The willow that bends in the wind survives; the willow that resists the wind will break.'

Over the centuries, the ideal was to create natural surroundings where the busy scholar or civil servant could meditate, write poetry, or practise his calligraphy. In this way he could continue his journey towards Tao without needing to travel to the mountains since *qi* develops from a relaxed and receptive mind in touch with nature. A suitable study pavilion was always incorporated into the garden's design. The rock piles simulated mountains and hid panoramic views so that the garden could gradually unfold its beauties in a series of pictures glimpsed through decorated grills or moon-shaped openings in the walls, while winding paths led to pavilion viewpoints or cool grottos. The garden was designed to change as the year progressed: each season would bring its special delights and

Taoism and Fung Shui

In China the earth is a sacred place, from the wells and the old trees in the villages, to the great mountain ranges. This view of the world is apparent in the ancient science of geomancy or, as it is known locally, *fung shui* (directly translated as 'wind water'). The earth is regarded as a living being, with lines of force known as 'dragon veins'. They follow the contours of the mountains and the *qi* accumulates in certain areas

風
水

so that those living there will benefit from the special cosmic energy. One such area is Central and, in particular, the site of the Hongkong and Shanghai Bank Building.

The art of finding auspicious

65

THE EIGHT SACRED SYMBOLS OF BUDDHISM

1. Conch shell symbolizing the voice of Buddha

2. Lotus symbolizing purity

3. Parasol symbolizing royal authority

4. Fish symbolizing spiritual liberalism

5. Vase symbolizing immortality

6. Halberd symbolizing victory

7. Endless Knot symbolizing the unity of all things

8. The Wheel of Life symbolizing the Eightfold Path that offers escape from the endless cycle of birth and rebirth

These eight symbols were traditionally inscribed on a representation of the imprint of Buddha's foot.

locations for houses or graves to benefit from landscape cosmic forces is very important in Hong Kong, as well as other countries where there is a strong Chinese presence. No business will move to other premises without consulting a *fung shui* master, who charges for his advice by the square foot of the property surveyed. New tall buildings that cast shadows over older buildings are considered particularly dangerous. The new Bank of China Building, designed by I. M. Pei, has been likened to a knife cutting through the *fung shui* of Government House below it. *Fung shui* experts believe that this is responsible for the many difficulties faced by the later governors of Hong Kong.

As in the case of crowded Hong Kong, where there is so little space, *fung shui* can still be enhanced or 'bad *fung shui*' neutralized. The birth dates and other elements of the residents of buildings examined are taken into consideration by the *fung shui* masters, and the interior decoration is harmonized to suit the individuals living or working there.

Buddhism

The last great religious force to influence the Chinese was Buddhism. It was founded in north-east India by Gautama Siddhartha (566–480 BC) from the Sakya tribe, and he is still known as Sakyamuni or 'The Sage of the Sakyas'. Siddhartha was born into a high-class ruling family, but, against the wishes of

Sakyamuni, Yin Hing Monastery, Lantau

the most important symbols of Buddhism. The Sanskrit word 'Buddha' means awakened or enlightened, and it was not until after his enlightenment at the age of thirty-four that Siddhartha came to be called Buddha.

Buddhist Beliefs (The Dharma)

On attaining enlightenment, Buddha explained the 'Four Noble Truths' and the 'Eightfold Path' which are at the heart of his teaching, and known as the *Dharma*. The Four Noble Truths are as follows:

1. Suffering consists of disease, old age, and death; separation from those we love; craving for what we cannot obtain; and hating what we cannot avoid.
2. All suffering is caused by desire and the attempt to satisfy our desires.
3. Therefore suffering can be overcome by ceasing to desire.
4. The way to end desire is to follow the Eightfold Path.

his father who feared losing the heir to his throne, he renounced his life of luxury and 'went forth from home with shaved head and begging bowl' in search of enlightenment and happiness.

After studying with two gurus, Siddhartha endured six years of harsh austerity and near starvation, until finally, he decided to forego also this way of life., Instead, eschewing all extremes, he adopted the 'Middle Way' which he felt was more likely to lead to enlightenment. This came to him after he had eaten a dish of milk rice and sat deep in meditation under the shade of a pipal tree for forty-nine days. This tree, thereafter named the bodhi or enlightenment tree, is one of

The Eightfold path is a series of stages that lead to the end of desire. Listed in ascending order of difficulty, the earlier ones attainable in everyday life, but the later ones require effort and meditation. The Eightfold Path comprises:

1. right opinion
2. right intentions
3. right speech
4. right conduct
5. right livelihood

67

6. right effort
7. right mindfulness
8. right concentration.

The basic Buddhist beliefs, which lead to enlightenment, are Samsara, Karma, Nirvana, and Sangha. Samsara, in Sanskrit, means 'perpetual wandering' which refers to the journey of the being through an infinite and unwelcome number of lives that can be lived in godly, human, or animal form. The doctrine of Karma teaches that doing good helps one to progress to a higher form in the next life, but bad deeds or evil thoughts will lead to rebirth in a lower life form.

According to this doctrine, every aspect of human life is dependent on previous decisions and actions, and so everything comes into existence on account of something else. In our ignorance, we crave to satisfy our egos and pander to our desires, but this inevitably leads to rebirth and, therefore, old age, illness, and death. It is only by giving up our illusion of being separate entities in a battle against the hostile outside universe that we can come to realize that there is no self to be trapped inside and no outside universe to be trapped by. Only then can we become truly free, that is, free of all self-concern and selfishness, and able to interact with others in a way that leads not to suffering, but to happiness.

Nirvana, in Sanskrit, means 'extinguishing' or 'blowing out', like the flames of a candle. Man's escape from the cycle of Karma can only be achieved by eliminating ourselves or our egos, and attaining a state of 'no self' where nothing remains to be reborn. Nirvana is the state of absolute peace, enlightenment, and compassion. It is impossible for the unenlightened mind to conceive it. This eternal, still emptiness can be compared with the Taoist *wu*, the silent non-being which is the source and basis of all things. It was this sense of absolute compassion that led Buddha to delay his own Nirvana so that he could teach other men the knowledge that would enable them too to find enlightenment.

From the earliest days when the five ascetics (with whom Siddhartha had earlier

Bodhisattva statues at the Po Lin Monastery, Lantau

shared his self-imposed sufferings) became his first followers, Buddha taught that the easiest way to Nirvana was through the religious community or Sangha. It is here that, in the absence of negative forces and in the quest for spiritual peace, the monk or nun can practise meditation to gain the tranquillity and awareness that may ultimately lead to Nirvana.

Chinese Buddhism

About 500 years after Buddha's death, a new school of thought grew up alongside the old. Those lay persons who were excluded from full participation in the Sangha became dissatisfied with the religious communities' self-centred search for Nirvana. This resulted in the Mahayana Movement which taught that all beings possessed the same innate ability as Buddha to reach Nirvana. It was believed that some people who, in their previous incarnation, were destined for enlightenment had followed Buddha's example and vowed not to enter Nirvana until they had led others there before them. These unselfish saints of Buddhism are called Bodhisattva. One of them was Avalokiteshvara or Kwan Yin in Chinese. When she was about to enter Nirvana, there was an uproar in the Heavens so, in a supreme act of compassion and generosity, the Bodhisattva drew back to continue working as saviour and guardian of mankind.

The older tradition, known as Theravada Buddhism, moved south, establishing itself in Sri Lanka from where it spread to Burma, Laos, Thailand, and Cambodia. The Mahayana tradition travelled northwards to Nepal and along the trading route known as the 'Silk Road', entering China some time in the first century AD. Intrepid monks made the long and dangerous journey between China and India to bring back knowledge of Buddhism and, in particular, the important writings or Sutras which they translated.

One of the best known and most loved stories in Chinese literature is *Journey to the West*. It is the story of a pilgrimage to India to recover the authentic scriptures of Buddhism 'so that they may be forever implanted in the East to enlighten the people'. The leader was Tripitaka, a disciple who had been expelled from Heaven for being inattentive during a sermon by Buddha. The other pilgrims were Monkey Sun, who had played havoc in Heaven with his naughty tricks; Pigsy, a pig who had flirted with the Moon Goddess while drunk; and Sandy, a monk who had broken a crystal cup at the heavenly feast. In their quest, they survived many ordeals and slew many evil demons, and it took the brave pilgrims fourteen

Monkey Sun, Tin Hau Temple, Stanley

years to complete the return journey and deliver the scriptures. Tripitaka and Monkey Sun eventually reached Nirvana. The story is so well loved that it is told everywhere, in opera, in puppet shows, in books and cartoons, and has even been shown on television in the UK. The acrobatic show 'Monkey Plays Tricks in Heaven' is performed all over China. You can find Monkey Sun standing on his hands in the temple at Stanley and he has his own complex of temples above Sau Mau Ping. The real Tripitaka may have been a Buddhist monk called Xuan Zang (AD 596–664) whose journey took seventeen years and who brought back 657 items of sacred text.

Buddhism reached the peak of its influence during the early part of the Tang dynasty (AD 618–907), and two distinctly Chinese forms of Buddhism emerged. Bodhidharma, or Da Mo in Chinese, founded the Chan sect. According to legend he arrived by ship from India around AD 520 and immediately created an impression—partly because of his holiness and partly because he was the ugliest man anyone had ever seen. He is still shown scowling in pictures and statues in Buddhist temples with bushy eyebrows and a beard. When he failed to impress the emperor, he floated across the Yellow River on a reed and took up residence at the monastery of Shao Lin Si, later famed for its martial arts. Here he sat in silent meditation for nine years on end staring at the wall until he was finally persuaded to impart his

wisdom. He taught that a person could reach Nirvana on his own through meditation, but that study of the scriptures alone would not lead to enlightenment. This strand of Buddhism survived the later Tang dynasty's persecutions, eventually making its way to Japan where it developed into Zen Buddhism.

The other form of Buddhism to survive was 'Pure Land' Buddhism. It taught that there were whole universes outside our world, each inhabited by Buddhas or Bodhisattvas, all preaching the same basic wisdom. It is these Buddhas that are portrayed around the walls in the Ten Thousand Buddhas Temple in Sha Tin. The best known of these worlds is an idyllic realm known as 'The Western Paradise', where fragrant rivers flow past bejewelled trees and flocks of brightly coloured birds sing sweet songs. But, more important, those given entry can constantly listen to the Buddha's teaching and so it is easier to attain Nirvana. This utopia is presided over by Amitabha (O Mi To Fat), whose name means 'Boundless Light', and people leading a good life who believe in him and ask for his aid, can go to this place in the afterlife.

As each universe goes through the cycles of death and rebirth, new Buddhas appear to resume the teachings, since on earth people are ignorant and stubborn and forget Buddha's teachings. So the future Buddha, called Maitreya (Mi Lo Fat), meaning 'Gentleness' and always

Maitreya, Tin Hau Temple, Sha Kong Tsuen

humanity, he was originally thought of as male, and in Tibetan Buddhism he acquired a female consort, 'White Tara'. By the tenth century AD, Chinese Buddhists had integrated the two into Kwan Yin, the Goddess of Mercy, who is usually depicted dressed all in white.

Buddhist Monasteries and Nunneries in Hong Kong

Buddhism still features very highly in Hong Kong with new monasteries being built and old ones refurbished and enlarged. Monks and nuns with shaved heads from local Buddhist monasteries can be seen on the streets of Hong Kong wearing grey, brown, or beige cotton cross-over jackets, loose grey trousers tucked into knee length socks, and thong sandals on their feet; they often carry matching cotton shoulder bags. The more colourful deep yellow- or orange-clad monks are likely to be Thai or Tibetan Buddhist monks. In order to become a monk or nun, they renounce their family name and shave their heads to symbolize the renunciation of ordinary life and their commitment to following the spiritual path. This requires them to take on a new religious identity, residing in a monastery and eating vegetarian food. Monks and nuns lead a simple life of study, meditation, and prayer.

portrayed as a stout, laughing Buddha, is waiting in Heaven to come to earth and continue Buddhist teachings once again.

The personal attendants of Sakyamuni, the founding Buddha, and the Bodhisattvas known to have attained Nirvana are known as Arhats or Lohans, and their statues are often found in Buddhist temples. But of all the Bodhisattvas, Kwan Yin (Avalokiteshvara) is the best loved and most often encountered in Hong Kong, in Taoist as well as Buddhist temples. Known as 'The Lord Who Looks Down', suggesting his loving care of

The gateway to a monastery is usually impressive and located some distance from the main temple so that visitors feel they are leaving the secular world and entering a 'pure land'. The path leads uphill to 'uplift the spirit'. In

STATUES IN BUDDHIST TEMPLES

1. Bodhisattva

Wei To or Veda is the Protector of monasteries and Buddhist books. He wears armour and carries a sword.

Wen Shu or Manjushri is the Bodhisattva of Wisdom. He is usually seated on a lion's back and carries a sword in one hand to fight ignorance, and a treatise of transcendental wisdom in the other.

Pu Xian or Samantabhadra is the Bodhisattva of Perfection. He is to be found seated on the back of an elephant and he carries a mace.

2. The Eighteen Lohans

These were the eighteen disciples of Buddha. They are often found in two rows of nine facing each other.

3. The Four Heavenly Kings

They are supernatural beings who traditionally guard the slopes of Paradise. In temples they can be seen guarding the entrance hall. They were originally Indian brothers but were given Chinese names:

Mo Li Chung carries a sword that can whip up a thousand spears to pierce the bodies of the enemy.

Mo Li Hai has a four-stringed guitar that produces music that will hold the enemy in thrall while their fortifications are being destroyed.

Mo Li Hung bears the Umbrella of Chaos which can stir up terrible earthquakes and storms and cover the earth in darkness.

Mo Li Shu has two whips and a sack containing a creature that can turn into a winged elephant when released from the bag.

larger Buddhist temples such as Chuk Lam Sin Yuen (Bamboo Monastery) there will be an entrance hall with the future Buddha, Maitreya (Mi Lo Fat), seated in the entrance smiling on all who arrive. He always holds a string of prayer beads each signifying one hundred years of waiting time and often he has a hemp bag which contains the original *qi*, the primal breath of creation. The four corners of the entrance hall are guarded by the four heavenly kings. Standing with his back to Maitreya and facing the main hall which he guards, is Wei To, the Bodhisattva who protects monasteries and Buddhist books. He is unmistakable in full armour and holding a drawn sword.

The main hall signifies its importance by its height and size. It is always built on a podium and approached up steps. Inside, the three Precious Buddhas will sit side by side. The founding Buddha, Sakyamuni, always sits in the middle. He may be accompanied by Ding Guang Fat, the Buddha of the past, on his right, and Maitreya, the Buddha of the future on his left. An alternative threesome consists of Sakyamuni with Yeuk Si Fat, the healing Buddha who rules over the Eastern Paradise, on his right, and Amitabha, the ruler of the Western Paradise, on his left. The hand positions of both sets will be the same. Sakyamuni points towards the ground since he is said to have called upon earth to bear witness to the truth of teachings. The Buddha on his right

Buddhist fish

holds his hands quietly in his lap as a sign that his work is complete, while the Buddha on his left will have one hand raised in a gesture of teaching. The pearl or dot in the middle of each Buddha's forehead signifies the third all-seeing eye that can see into the hearts of supplicants. A swastika engraved on the chest of a Buddha is the symbol or seal of Buddha's heart and the Chinese character for it denotes the 10,000 blessings Buddha can bestow. The Buddhas sit on lotus flower thrones since the lotus represents innocence and purity. On the altar on the right of the three Precious Buddhas you will find a hollow wooden object with a wide mouth-like slit. This is a Buddhist fish and it is struck during prayers to maintain the rythm of the chants.

Somewhere in every monastery and usually standing behind a screen with her back to Sakyamuni you will find Kwan Yin, the best loved of the Bodhisattvas. She is often shown with a willow branch in her hand with which she sprinkles healing water on the sick. Willow is the symbol of feminine beauty and the weeping willow symbolizes her compassionate concern for the ills of this world. Kwan Yin may hold a vase, the symbol of peace, from which to dispense mercies or the Lotus Sutra which refers to the origin of her powers.

All monasteries, whether Taoist or Buddhist will have a number of halls where, for a sum of money, the ashes of the deceased can be deposited in a 'locker' in the wall with its own inscription and perhaps a picture. The family can then visit and pay their respects at the appropriate times of the year. The dead soul will benefit from the prayers of the monks and the holiness of the site. Many monasteries also provide a place of refuge for the elderly to live out their lives in peace.

Chinese Popular Religion in Hong Kong

You might think that in a modern, capitalistic city like Hong Kong, with a population brought up on a Western, science-orientated curriculum, popular religion, inherited from days gone by, would be on the decline. However, you will find that this is far from true. The signs of the prevalence of popular religion are all around. Temples, both Taoist and Buddhist, are continually renovated while new temples are built. Major religious festivals are always well attended: over 100,000 worshippers visited the temple of Che Kung at Shatin on or around the second day of Chinese New Year in 1996. Even greater numbers paid their respects at the Wong Tai Sin temple. The dense crowds of worshippers, pushing and jostling to place their joss sticks in the incense burners, felt more like an MTR station platform in the rush hour. Between 20,000 and 30,000 people turn out to help celebrate the birthday of the Hakka boy god, Tam Kung, in Shau Kei Wan every year, and, on the birthday of Tin Hau, the Goddess of the Sea, the main Tin Hau temples are packed to overflowing. The temples, whether Taoist or Buddhist, are the outward signs of the continuing importance of popular religion in the lives of the local people.

Tin Hau Temple, Fong Ma Po

When foreigners enter a Chinese temple they sometimes feel overwhelmed and intimidated. The strangeness of the smoke-blackened gods, the relentless redness of the walls, pillars, and roof, and the ambiguous actions of the worshippers are very alien to Western religious practices.

The main difference between Chinese temples and Christian churches is that the temples are the residences of the gods and not centres of group worship. Anyone with an affinity for a particular god can worship in that god's own place of abode and pray to him through act of devotion known in Cantonese as *paai shan*. This is done by lighting joss sticks, bowing low before the god's shrine, and making an offering of specially prepared paper goods that will be burnt in the temple furnace. Offerings of oranges, cakes, or roast meat are also common gifts for the god to enjoy. Joss sticks are burnt in bundles of three, which represent the triad of *Tin* (Heaven), *Dei* (earth), and *Yan* (humanity).

For the most part, Chinese religions do not believe that the layman requires intermediaries to help him get in touch with the gods. Most Taoist temples, therefore, do not have priests in residence. The larger and more prosperous temples are maintained by lay temple keepers and small temples are often cared for by devout elderly pensioners. Taoist priests are needed on occasions when complicated rituals are to be performed and long passages of scripture have to be memorized. They perform at funerals and at ceremonies to bless new homes, exorcise ghosts, or heal the sick. They often work as makers of the paper goods that are burnt at the time of the funeral to provide for the newly departed soul in Heaven.

The Gods

Chinese popular religion has a pantheon of gods in much the same way as the Greeks and Romans, with the Jade Emperor as the head of the Chinese hierachy. He rules, in the manner of any Chinese Emperor, over a court of heavenly officials composed of gods of different ranks. The Jade Emperor mediates between the often conflicting petitions of his officials and keeps his entourage in order. At Chinese New Year, all the gods pay their respects to the Jade Emperor, including the Kitchen Gods.

Chinese gods were originally mortals who, due to their exemplary lives or their particular powers, were given the gift of immortality and who prove their efficacy by performing miracles after their deaths. Worshippers believe that there is a strong reciprocal relationship between the worshipper and the god. If one has the attention of the god and offers him the sweet scent of incense and offerings of fruit or expensive food, the god is obliged to listen to the devotee, and offer help and advice in solving problems. The gods can in some ways be likened to

HONG KONG GODS

The Jade Emperor

He is king of heaven and supreme deity in charge of the heavenly hierarchy of gods. He lives in the constellation of stars known as the Great Bear with the star gods, Fuk, Luk, and Sau—the gods of happiness, affluence, and long life.

Pak Tai

His full title is 'Superior Divinity of the Deep Dark Heaven, True Soldier of the North'. He is linked to the time before history when the Demon King was ravaging the universe and the Gods felt bound to intervene. Shang Ti, the Primordial Deity, ordered the Jade Emperor to appoint Pak Tai Commander-in-chief and send him to do battle against the hordes of the Demon King. Dressed in black robes and a golden breastplate, Pak Tai fought bare-footed which is why in his statues he is portrayed as shoeless. After his victory over the Demon King and his evil hordes which included a magic snake and a tortoise, he was rewarded with the title of First Lord of Heaven. He is often to be seen with the snake and tortoise under his foot. Temples dedicated to him can be found on Lung On Street in Wan Chai, and on Cheung Chau.

Kwan Ti

Kwan Ti, also known as Kwan Yu or Kwan Kung, is the red-faced God of War. He is patron to the police and other uniformed branches in Hong Kong because of his courage, loyalty, and incredible reputation as a warrior. He is a historic character whose eventful and exciting story is told in one of the earliest Chinese novels, *Romance of the Three Kingdoms*. He was beheaded in AD 219 after a treacherous betrayal. He is always shown with a long black beard and holding a halberd.

Man Cheong

Emperor Man Cheong is the Civil God and God of Literature, worshipped by those with examinations to pass. He is said to have been born in AD 287 and held jurisdiction over civil servants in the Jin Dynasty. He is still said to govern the destinies of civil servants. The title of emperor was conferred on him during the Yuan Dynasty. He can be found paired with Kwan Ti at the Man Mo temples in Hollywood Road and Tai Po, and at the Yi Tai study hall in Kam Tin.

Tin Hau

Tin Hau is perhaps the most important goddess in the Territory with more than forty temples dedicated to her. Her birthday which is celebrated on the twenty-third day of the third moon (Chinese almanac) is the occasion for celebrations all round the territory and particularly in Junk Bay and Yuen Long. She was born into a poor Fujian family who made their living from the sea. When still a child, she dreamt that her father and two brothers were in great danger of drowning in a terrible storm at sea. In her dream she was in the process of dragging their three boats to safety when her mother woke her with a start and she let go of one of the ropes. The two brothers arrived home with the story of a beautiful girl who had towed them to safety. Sadly their father in the third boat had drowned.

Tin Hau died young and unmarried. Ever since, there have been numerous stories of her appearance at crucial moments of peril to render assistance to seafarers. She was promoted to Queen of Heaven in 1683 after she helped the Chinese navy regain control of Taiwan.

Tam Kung, the Hakka Boy God
Tam Kung was a peasant boy from Wai Dung county in Guangdong Province, north of Hong Kong. He lived in the thirteenth century and was famed for his healing powers, but he died young. He was friendly with tigers and is often portrayed followed by a tiger and holding a basket of medicine. He was brought to Hong Kong by migrating Hakka

people about one hundred years ago. Besides healing, Tam Kung also specialized in weather control. By throwing up a cupful of peas, he could quell a typhoon, while by substituting water for the peas in the cup, he could cause a downpour that would put out a raging fire. His birthday, on the eighth day of the fourth moon, is celebrated particularly in Shau Kei Wan and Macau when the 'Dance of the Drunken Dragon' is held.

Hau Wong, Prince Marquis
Hau Wong is a very local deity with temples dedicated to him at Kowloon City, Tai O, and Tung Chung. His story dates from the end of the Song dynasty when the last remaining emperor, a boy of eight, fled from the Mongol invaders to take refuge in Kowloon and Lantau. The forces of the young emperor were defeated in a final battle to the south of Hong Kong. The court then left on a last journey on which the young boy drowned (suicide being preferable to capture). The devoted leader of his bodyguard, a man named Yeung Hau Wong, was too ill to accompany the court, so was left behind to fight a rearguard action and delay any pursuit. He died soon after, but he so impressed the locals with his loyalty, courage, and honesty that he was awarded the posthumous title of Prince Marquis. Temples dedicated to

him are sometimes called Hau Wong and sometimes Yeung Hau, perhaps so that the incoming Manchu rulers would not realize that local people were keeping alive memories of the Song opposition.

Hung Shing Kung

Although Hung Shing is a very popular deity in Hong Kong, with many temples (such as those at Ap Lei Chau and Queen's Road East) dedicated to him, very little is known about him. One story places him in the Tang dynasty when he was supposed to have been an exceptionally good government official in the Guangdong Province with a special gift for forecasting the weather. He is certainly known as a god of the sea and patron of seafarers, and another story claims that he is really the Dragon King who rules the Southern Sea, helping all those who venture out on it.

Che Kung

Che Kung is supposed to have lived in the Song dynasty. He was a

military commander and because of his affinity with medicine, he is revered as a curer of diseases and epidemics. His temple is in Sha Tin.

Kam Fa

Kam Fa is a local deity who is said to have lived in Guangdong. She was a wise old woman renowned for her abilities to heal, especially diseases of the eyes. She became linked to child-bearing and is responsible for health and safety during pregnancy.

Kwan Yin

Kwan Yin (or Kwun Yam) is a Bodhisattva and the Goddess of Mercy. She can be seen at Sha Tin's Ten Thousand Buddha Temple, the Chuk Lam Sin Yuen Monastery in Tsuen Wan, Po Lin Monastery on Lantau, and at the temple dedicated to her in Tai Ping Shan Street, Chai Wan.

the saints of the Catholic Church. Kwan Ti is the Patron God of the uniformed services such as the police and fire services. Kam Fa is the Goddess of Expectant Mothers, while Marshal Chao Kung Ming is the God of Wealth who brings luck to gamblers! This pantheon of gods is not static. In

Taiwan, Che Gong (Che Kung in Cantonese) has been adopted as the God of Cars.

The popularity of certain gods differs throughout China. Wong Tai Sin, who is considered so powerful in Hong Kong, is almost unknown in Beijing. The gods are not, as in the

Wong Tai Sin, Ling To Monastery

Christian faith, the epitome of various virtues, but are more like the wily Greek Gods. In the words of the anthropologist Dr. H Baker they are 'fickle, gullible, tricky, and prone to put self interest first'.

Each temple is dedicated to a main god whose statue stands in the central hall directly facing the doors. The bigger temples also have side altars that include other gods, since this is a means of increasing the popularity of the temple. Probably the most popular deity in Hong Kong is Tin Hau, the Queen of Heaven and patron Goddess of the Sea and all who work on the sea. She is easy to recognize as she often wears a headdress of hanging strands of pearls and is usually accompanied by her two special companions, Favourable Wind Ear, who can hear across a distance of a thousand *li* (500 kilometres), and Thousand *Li* Eye, who can see as far. There are more temples in Hong Kong dedicated to Tin Hau than to any other god.

One aspect of local beliefs borrowed from Buddhism is the belief in an underworld, where the soul does penance for evil deeds committed in life. At the Tin Hau temple complex in Yau Ma Tei, the second hall to the left is devoted to the ten gods of the underworld, each one in charge of one hall and each hall devoted to one particular 'class' of evil. There are very explicit pictures on the walls of the temple to show what horrible kinds of treatment await the soul in each hall.

The Tiger Balm Gardens on Tai Hang Road is another place where you can see the Underworld and many other legends of the immortals and gods in sculptured form.

Temples

On approaching a temple always look up at the roof ridge. The wealthier temples are generally decorated with a frieze of Shekwan pottery figures depicting dragons, carp, or human characters from Chinese mythology. The Shekwan potteries are situated at Foshan about one hour's drive from Guangzhou. Foshan has a beautiful old temple as well as the pottery works and is well worth a visit if you are in Guangdong. Recent archeological findings indicate that pottery has been produced in this area since the Tang dynasty.

Chai mun, *Yeung Hau Temple, Tung Tau Tsuen*

The courtyard of the temple is often guarded by a pair of lions. Lions were probably introduced into China from India with Buddhism, and they represent courage and loyalty, the two most valuable virtues of guardians. The male stands on the right with a ball under his paw—supposedly a giant pearl for him to play with. The female lion has a cub under one paw. The paintings over the door and the plaster decorations under the eaves on either side of the doors are often colourful and full of symbolic significance. A boat-shaped carving called a *chai mun* (literally 'colourful doorway') may be found over the doors of older, wealthier temples. They are often very finely carved with scenes of men and gods taken from mythology.

On the inside of the main doors are pictures of the guardian generals, painted in many different colours and styles, and with great precision and detail. Just inside the temple, spanning the width of the of the main doorway,

are the spirit doors. This second pair of doors, as in the clan halls, keeps out ghosts and evil spirits who can only travel in straight lines, and therefore cannot circumvent the second pair of doors. It does not matter if you find these doors open, as they often are, since the framework below the door itself is sufficiently high to deter malicious spirits.

Directly behind the spirit doors is the light well open to the skies so that the gods can see the heavens. It also allows light to enter the temple and smoke from the incense to escape. The great coils of incense that burn for days are paid for by individuals who wish to summon the gods to grant favours.

The burning of incense dates back several thousand years when the Emperors Yao, Shun, and Yu offered burnt offerings to Shang Ti, the Supreme Ruler and Ancestor. Emperor Yu, the last of these three, is said to have founded China's first dynasty, the Xia dynasty (c. 2100–1600 BC).

Inside, the temples are predominantly red, a colour that signifies happiness; the abode of gods must be a happy place. The other colours you will see are green for peace, and yellow for wealth and power. Temples never have windows because any unguarded aperture is a weak point through which harmful spirits may enter and disturb the

80

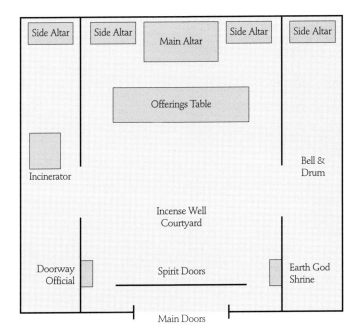

atmosphere of peace. The main altar of every temple always holds a set of altar furnishings, which consist of a central incense burner flanked on either side by a candle holder and a flower vase. The cover of the incense burner often depicts a lion, while the flower vases may hold floral decorations made of paper.

To one side of the temple, usually the right side, you will find the temple bell and the drum. The bell is often the oldest item in the temple and its inscription includes the date the temple was built. Chinese bells, unlike other types of bells, are struck from the outside when rung. Some bells, particularly in temples near the sea, are in the shape of an anchor. The temple

furnace is found either near the left-hand wall of the temple or outside in the courtyard. When a worshipper burns paper money or gold in the temple furnace for the gods, the gong and the bell are struck to signal to them that money is being sent.

The atmosphere in Chinese temples is much more relaxed than in a Christian church. It is quite natural and acceptable for temples to be used for other activities. It is not uncommon to find the temple keeper's clothes hanging up to dry, cleaning cloths spread out to air over an incense burner, or the temple keeper asleep on a camp bed having an afternoon nap. I once found a Sunday *mah jong* session taking place in a side room off the

Hau Wong Temple, Tung Chung

main temple. In the past the local primary schools were often situated in or next to the temple, and accommodation for visitors used to be provided in a room attached to the building. In the Man Mo temple at Tai Po one room was used by the official in charge of weights and measures. His role was to arbitrate disputes using the official scales and these are still traditionally kept in the temple.

Divination
In front of the temple's main altar is a red table, usually holding offerings. In larger temples you will find on a corner of the table small blocks of wood in pairs shaped like two half moons, often called 'Buddha's lips'. Each half has one flat (*yin*) side and

one curved (*yang*) side. When they are thrown to the ground by the worshipper these blocks reveal the god's answer: if both blocks fall flat side down, the answer is an unequivocal 'no'; if they both fall on the curved side, the rocking motion of the blocks indicates that the god is laughing at the question. But if the blocks fall with one curved side up and one curved side down, then the answer to the question is 'yes'.

Also on the table you will see bamboo containers called *chim* filled with flat sticks of bamboo about the length of a chopstick. These holders usually contain either sixty-four or one hundred sticks, each of which is numbered. The worshipper kneels in front of the god he seeks direction from and makes his offerings. Concentrating deeply, he then asks the god questions, while shaking the container at a tilt. Gradually, one of the sticks will

'Buddha's lips' and chim *sticks, Hau Wong Temple, Tung Chung*

Kitchen God shrine, Fan Sin Temple, Wun Yin

Earth God shrine, Tap Mun Chau

Earth God shrine, Tai O

Tree God shrine, San Tin

Confucius lecturing on the Apricot Terrace by Wu Bin

Taoist monks contemplating the sunrise

*The Three Precious Buddhas, Tsing
Shan Monastery, Tuen Mun*

*Hanging Kesi slit tapestry of the Eight
Immortals*

Golden pagodas near Ling To Monastery

Graves on the hillside, Ha Wo Hang

Yuen Yuen Institute, Tsuen Wan

Roof with phoenixes, Tsing Shan Monastery, Tuen Mun

Ching Chung Koon Monastery, Tuen Mun

Kwan Ti (left) and Man Cheong, Man Mo Temple, Tai Po

Tin Hau, Tin Hau Temple, Lung Yeuk Tau

Kam Fa, Yeung Hau Temple, Tung Tau Tsuen

Kwan Yin at the Dajiao ceremony, Nga Tsin Wai, Kowloon

Hung Shing Kung, Hang Mei Tsuen

Hau Wong Temple, Tai O

Che Kung Temple, Ho Po, Sai Kung

Roof ridge, Tsing Shan Monastery, Tuen Mun

Ching Chung Koon Monastery, Tuen Mun

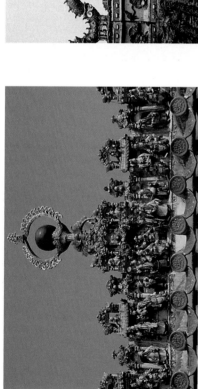

Roof ridge, Tin Hau Temple, Tap Mun Chau

Chai mun, Tin Hau Temple, Tap Mun Chau

Hau Wong Temple, Tung Chung

the brook which flowed through the royal pavilion. A scholar called Yu Yau happened upon one and responded. This communication of love poems continued for ten years until the maid was finally given her freedom by the emperor and allowed to marry her faithful scholar. The story's message is that if life is lived with patience and propriety, good fortune will finally be enjoyed.

Another example of one of these messages is, 'So Mo was made to look after the sheep'. So Mo was a high official in the Han dynasty (206 BC–AD 220), who was sent as an ambassador to a barbaric northern king. This king forced So Mo to take care of a male sheep, vowing not to release him until the sheep gave birth. The ambassador, with no food or water, was reduced to eating ice and sheep's wool, until finally, after nineteen long years, So Mo was allowed to return home. This story forecasts much suffering in the immediate future, but suggests that the hard times will eventually pass.

separate and fall to the ground. The number on the stick can be matched with a message containing words of advice obtained from a board or the temple keeper. These messages are based on Chinese mythology and history and may need interpreting by a fortune teller or the temple keeper.

One message that the worshipper may find is, 'Red leaves float along the royal ditch'. This comes from the story of a maid tied to serving in the court of a Tang emperor. She wrote love poems on red leaves and floated them down

PART 2

Trips to the New Territories & Outlying Islands

CHAPTER 1

THE PING SHAN HERITAGE TRAIL

This interesting and enjoyable trail, about one kilometre long, was set up by the Antiquities and Monuments Office to link together a number of traditional buildings so that they could be seen on a half-day excursion.

The route takes the visitor through the villages of Hang Mei Tsuen and Hang Tau Tsuen and to the walled village of Sheung Cheung Wai. Signposts and information boards have been put up at convenient locations to help visitors appreciate what they see. This area was chosen for the first heritage trail not only because of the number of interesting buildings but also because of its very long history. One branch of the powerful Tang clan settled here as long ago as the twelfth century. It was due to the consent and cooperation of the Tangs that this trail has been opened, and those following the trail are asked to respect the local

people and keep disturbance to a minimum. A trail guide with more details can be bought at all tourist offices.

If you come by car you will need to turn off Castle Peak Road on to Ping Ha Road, crossing the LRT track at the traffic lights where the Ping Shan Heritage Trail is signposted. Continue about a mile down Ping Ha Road through the village. Two possible

Hung Shing Temple, Hang Mei Tsuen

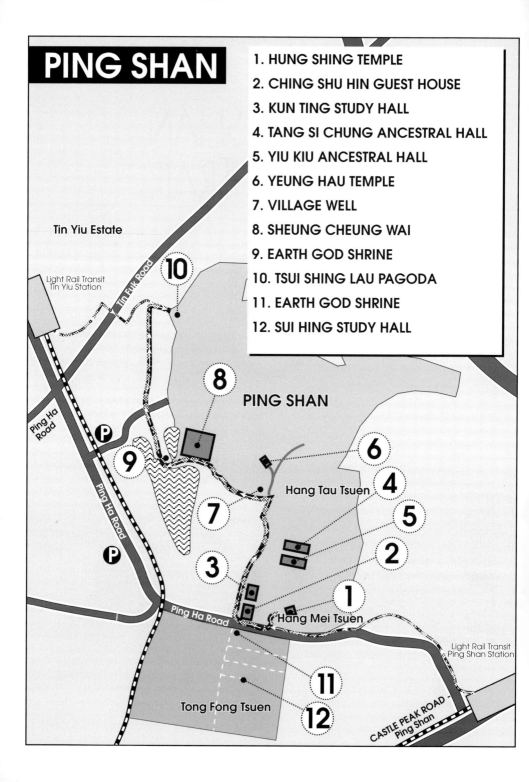

parking areas are marked on the map off Tin Yiu Road. Having parked the car walk back up the road, passing the sign on the left for the heritage trail, and continue walking up the hill until you come to a small garden square with the **Hung Shing Temple** in the top left-hand corner. The trail begins here.

If you arrive by LRT (Light Rail Transit), a pleasant five-minute walk down Ping Ha Road will bring you to the garden square of Hang Mei Tsuen and the Hung Shing Temple. After viewing the temple continue down Ping Ha Road to the right-hand turning where the trail is marked. As you round the corner you will be walking alongside the outside wall of the **Ching Shu Hin Guest House**. The first building beyond it on the right is the **Kun Ting study hall.** Both these buildings were constructed around 1870 to show off the power and prestige of the Tang clan and are

Ching Shu Hin Guest House with the Kun Ting study hall beyond

perhaps the finest examples of their type in the territory. The British requisitioned this guest house soon after the New Territories were leased to them in 1898 for the use of local administative officer, James Stewart Lockhart. Sadly, they are both closed to the public, due to a dispute between elders of the Tang clan and the Government over the removal of ancestral grave sites (see page 52).

If you turn up the tiny passageway between the two buildings you can catch tantalizing glimpses of the guesthouse interior through the small windows, and, as you turn back, the colourful mouldings on the doorway and at the corner of the study hall can be seen. If the imposing doors with their lion-head handles were open, you would see the rich interior decorated by some of the most skilful craftsmen of the period. The ancestral altar and its surrounds are carved and painted. Elegant screens and doorways depicting bamboos and flowers close off study rooms on either side. The roof brackets and beams are finely carved. The atmosphere is harmonious and tranquil.

Continue down the road until you come into a wide market square looking out over the former paddy fields. Notice, in the sitting-out and play area in front of the fields, the canon, perhaps last used when the Tang clan, among others, took up arms in 1898 against the British takeover of the New Territories.

On the opposite side of the square are two imposing clan halls. On the left

Tang Si Chung ancestral hall

is the older of the two, the **Tang Si Chung ancestral hall**. If you had thought that nothing in Hong Kong was much older than a hundred years you will be surprised. According to clan records, this hall was built by Tang Fung Shun, of the fifth generation about 700 years ago. The twenty-fifth generation has now reached adulthood and the twenty-sixth generation is growing up. Before you go in, notice the two drum platforms on either side of the entrance for musicians to play during festivities. Take a look, also, at the roof ridge with the Shekwan pottery dragon fish (see page 44) and a unicorn at each corner, peeping out from under the gable edge. The outer columns of red sandstone show the wealth of the clan and inside the first courtyard, the unique (in Hong Kong) raised red sandstone pathway indicates that a Tang clansman was a high-ranking mandarin in the Imperial

Government.

When you enter the hall, be sure to examine the roof with its beams and brackets, all finely carved with auspicious Chinese motives. As is usual, the ancestral tablets are displayed at the far end of the hall. In both halls you will see good examples of green and blue grille tiles used in the windows instead of glass. They ensure a certain privacy but allow a current of air to pass through the rooms. The coin motif depicts good fortune. The **Yu Kiu ancestral hall** to the right of the Tang hall was constructed early in the sixteenth century by two brothers of the eleventh generation. The layout and design is identical to that of the Tang Si Chung hall.

Outside the two halls are several pairs of upright **scholar stones** erected to honour Tang clansman who passed the Imperial Civil Service Examination (see page 32). The names of the successful candidates, carved on the slabs, are now mostly illegible.

Go back across the square, leaving the halls behind you, and turn right. You will now be in the village of Hang Tau Tsuen. At the fork you will see a signpost pointing to Sheung Cheung Wai on the left. First take the right-hand path, then turn left up the narrow track to reach the **Yeung Hau Temple** dedicated to Hau Wong. The side bays of this temple house statues to Kam Fa, Patron Saint of Expectant Mothers, on the left, and, on the right, an altar to To Tei, the Earth God.

Returning to the fork in the lane, take the other path, which will lead you past the old village well. It is probably more than two hundred years old and once served as the main source of drinking water for this end of the village.

Continuing down the path, you will come to **Sheung Cheung Wai**, a walled village, built about two hundred years ago. The gatehouse with its shrine is still intact. The main path through the centre of the village leads to the small temple at the far end. If you walk along it, you can still see some old traditional houses in the narrow lanes that branch off to the left and right. Once outside the village again, turn right and continue along the concrete path. You will pass a fine example of an **Earth God Shrine** with *wok yee-*shaped sides, so called because they resemble the handles of a wok. It lies peacefully beside the *fung shui* pond which gives Sheung Cheung Wai a more prosperous outlook.

Continue along the path beyond the shrine, disregarding the fact that it becomes progressively less enticing, with a large

housing estate in front of you and gravelled lorry parks on the right. Finally your perseverance will be rewarded by the sight of Hong Kong's only antique pagoda down a short path on the right-hand side of the track

Again, according to local records, this three-storied octagonal pagoda, **Tsui Shing Lau**, 'The Pagoda of Gathering Stars' (No. 5 on the north-west New Territories Countryside Series map) was built by a seventh-generation Tang more than 600 years ago for *fung shui* purposes, and is auspiciously in alignment with Castle Peak. It was built to counter destructive influences from the north (probably flooding and evil spirits) and to ensure the clan success in the Imperial Examinations, and it seems to have very successfully fulfilled its role. It is said to have originally had seven floors but, after the upper stories twice collapsed, perhaps in typhoons, the geomancers agreed that it was better to

Earth God Shrine

91

PUBLIC TRANSPORT	
KMB	
53	Tsuen Wan Ferry to Yuen Long East via Ping Ha Road
64M	Tsuen Wan Ferry Pier to Tin Shui Wai
69M	Kwai Fong MTR station to Tin Shui Wai
276	Tin Shui Wai to Sheung Shui
Public Light Buses (Green)	
33	Tai Fung Street, Yuen Long to Lower Pak Nai
34	Tai Fung Street, Yuen Long to Lau Fau Shan
35	Tai Fung Street, Yuen Long to Tsim Bei Tsui
LRT	
610, 614, & 615	Yuen Long Terminus to Ferry Pier Terminus, Tuen Mun (Ping Shan Station)
721	Tin Shui Wai Terminus to Yuen Long Terminus (Ping Shan and Tin Yiu Stations)
LRT feeder bus	
655	Yuen Long Terminus to Lau Fau Shan via Ping Ha Road

leave it as it now stands. On the top floor, there used to be a statue to Fui Shing, the deity in control of success and failure in examinations.

This is the end of the tour and you can now retrace your steps to the car park. Alternatively, if you want to catch a bus or LRT, you should take the path up the embankment and cross over Tin Fuk Road by the bridge. Turn left, and continue round to join Tin Yiu Road. Slightly further along is the Tin Yiu LRT station and beside the station is the bus stop.

ADDITIONAL PLACES OF INTEREST IN THE PING SHAN AREA

There are at least four very interesting buildings to be found very close to the Heritage Trail. They make it well worth visiting the area again for further exploration. The first is within a stone's throw of the heritage trail and can easily be combined with it.

1. The Pai-lau from the former Shut Hing Study Hall
The village of Tong Fong Tsuen lies on the other side of the Ping Ha Road. Cross the road and enter the village

immediately opposite Hang Mei Tsuen where the Heritage Trail begins. You will pass another Earth God Shrine on the left of the turning.

Walk into the village and take the third small lane to the left. You will suddenly come face to face with this amazing structure. A *pai-lau* is a memorial to a distinguished person. This one formerly divided the two parts of the Shut Hing study hall, which was demolished in 1977 to make way for modern housing. Thus, this splendid gateway, with its huge guardian generals, leads nowhere. It is without doubt the most impressive *pai-lau* in Hong Kong. The entire front is very decorative with carved wooden friezes, elegant stone guardian lions, auspicious painted plaster mouldings and Shekwan pottery figures. It is well worth a small detour to see it (No. 6 on the north-west New Territories Countryside Series map).

Tang Si Chung clan hall

2. Tang Si Chung Clan Hall in Ha Tsuen Shi

About two kilometres further on down the Ping Ha Road, you will come to the village of Ha Tsuen Shi. From the heritage trail, follow Ping Ha Road to the junction turning right as if to Tin Shui Wai, then taking the left-hand turning towards Lau Fau Shan, passing under a bridge. Continue straight on at the traffic lights following the Ping Ha Road's winding course. After passing a couple of immense container parks, you will see the village of Ha Tsuen Shi, which lies a little back from the road on the left-hand side. You can either park in the forecourt of the clan hall itself, or, if you miss that, take the first turning to the left which leads to Sik Kong Wai, where you will find a parking space. This clan hall was built in 1751 to serve the needs of the Tang villages round Ha Tsuen. A large iron cannon, dug up in 1979, has been placed on one of the drum terraces.

Inside the clan hall, take a look at the roof. The finely carved wooden beams are supported on equally well-carved wooden brackets. Notice the two large boards on either side of the hall where, in elegant calligraphy, Tang clansmen are exhorted to follow the Confucian principles of *hau,* filial piety, and *tai,* fraternal love. A series of smaller boards painted red and stored in a rack on the left-hand side of the temple, proclaim the examination successes of the local Tang clansmen. The ancestral tablets, at the far end of the hall, are housed in a very finely carved altar surround.

Altar carving, Yeung Hau temple

If you take a walk on either side of the hall, but particularly on the right-hand side (when facing the clan hall), you can still find some old-style houses with interesting painted plaster mouldings over the doorways.

3. *Yeung Hau Temple in Tung Tau Tsuen*

One kilometre further down Ping Ha Road is the village of Tung Tau Tsuen which boasts one of the finest temples in the New Territories. Continue until you see a large pond on the left, then park in the nearest off-street parking area. The village lies a little way back from the road, so take the footpath that borders the pond which is signposted to Yeung Hau Temple and to Tung Tau Tsuen.

This temple, with its distinctive red sandstone pillars and drum platforms on either side of the doors, is well worth searching out. It is said to be about two hundred years old and is dedicated to Hau Wong (see page 77) It

was erected by the Tang clan members of the three closest villages known locally as Tung Tau Sam Tsuen or, the 'Three Villages of the East', and is carefully situated with Lion Head Hill, a *fung shui* wood behind, and a spacious courtyard, now used as a playground, in front. It is likened in *fung shui* terms to a lion playing with a ball, the hill being the lion and the temple, the ball.

Before you go in, take a look at the roof ridge. Two stylized dragons enclose the decorated central part of the ridge. The sides of the roof have elegantly decorated, pointed gable ends. As you enter, notice the gold-painted, wooden, boat-shaped *chai mun* hanging over the entrance. Just inside, the screen doors are very attractive with auspicious bamboos and flowers painted on a white background. The main altar to Hau Wong in the centre has lively, and very realistic scenes carved and painted on its wooden surrounds. Be sure not to miss the pink-clad girls in their boat in mountainous seas, one rowing and the other perhaps beating a drum to scare the fish into the nets. The two other altars house the statues of Kam Fa, Patron Saint of Expectant Mothers (left), and To Dei, the Earth God (right).

To the right of the main hall, is an annex built later to house an altar to the two Mandarins, Chou and Wong, whose pleadings with the emperor led to the lifting of the Evacuation Order of 1662 and allowed the people of the area to return to their ravaged homes (see page ?). Altogether this temple is one you should not miss.

Ling To Monastery

4. Ling To Monastery

To reach Ling To Monastery (No. 1 on the north-west New Territories Countryside Series map) turn left off Ping Ha Road into Tin Ha Road. After about a kilometre, turn right along a narrow road signposted to San Sam Tsuen. Follow the road through the village and when you come to a junction take the right fork alongside the derelict Shiu Wah Dyeing and Textile Mill. The monastery is at the end of this road.

Ling To Monastery is small and little known but very peaceful and beautiful with a very long history. It was originally established further up the hill in the Tang Dynasty as a retreat for the monk Pui To (see page 143). It lies beside a stream with a shady pool where Pui To is said to have bathed.

The two main altars facing each other across a light well, have Buddhist Gods while the side altars on the other two sides of the well are dedicated to Kwan Ti and Wong Tai Sin respectively. The monastery possesses some very fine and interesting calligraphy including some by the famous calligrapher who commanded the Kowloon Walled City in the late nineteenth century. During the Second World War nearby villagers were suspected of aiding the guerrilla fighters and Japanese troops were sent to punish them. The villagers took refuge in the monastery and its heavenly guardians sent so many spirits to guard the narrow path that the soldiers took fright and turned back before discovering the monastery, never to return. During the grim years of the war and after, up to fifty children from the local villages would play there and I was told by one of those children that the resident monk would use his precious sugar to bake them cakes.

PUBLIC TRANSPORT	
KMB	
53	Tsuen Wan ferry to Yuen Long East via Tin Hai Road (alight at San Sang Tsuen)

CHAPTER 2

THE KAM TIN AREA

Kam Tin dates back to AD 1069 when Tang Hon Fu (see page 37) settled in the fertile valley and marked the importance of learning for the younger members of the Tang clan by building a study hall. Known originally as Shum Tin, Kam Tin's name was changed due to a terrible drought in 1587 in neighbouring Bao An county. The government granaries were empty and a call for help went practically unheeded until Tang Yuen Fan donated 1,000 piculs of rice. The magistrate from Boa An thereupon renamed the area 'Kam Tin', meaning 'fields of gold'. Kam Tin is still a goldmine with its rich heritage of study halls and clan halls. A heritage trail is being planned around this area which certainly deserves to be better known.

Kam Tin is approached from Shek Kong along the Kam Tin Road that leads to Yuen Long. Kam Tin consists of a cluster of villages which includes

five *wai*. **Kat Hing Wai** ('Village of Good Fortune') is the best known since its fortifications are by far the most complete. Driving from Shek Kong you will come to the walled village about one kilometre after you pass the airstrip; it is quite unmistakable on the left-hand side of the road, just as the houses begin to thin out. You can turn in and park your car in the open area in front of the narrow gateway.

The village is much visited and well used to tourists. It was built between 1465 and 1487, and the walls and surrounding moat were added between 1662 and 1721 to protect the inhabitants from marauding bandits and pirates with gun towers at each corner and gun slots along the walls. The present cast-iron gates were taken to Ireland by the governor, Sir Henry Blake, as a war trophy after the resistance to British rule had been

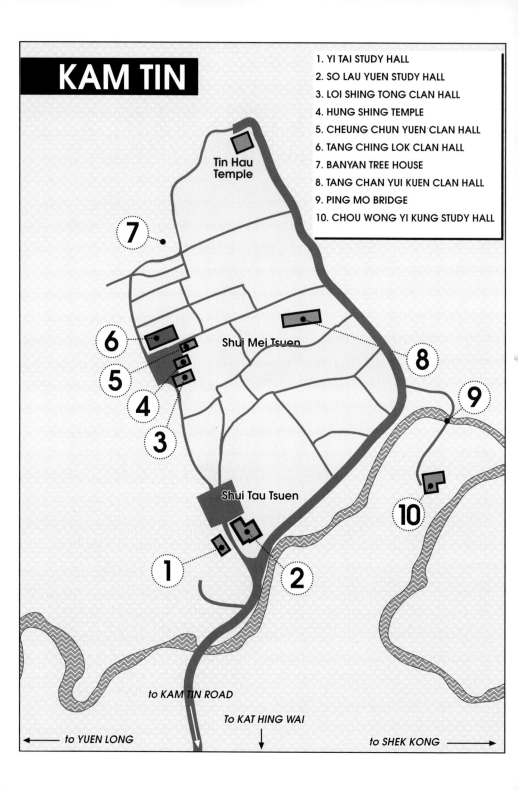

KAM TIN

1. YI TAI STUDY HALL
2. SO LAU YUEN STUDY HALL
3. LOI SHING TONG CLAN HALL
4. HUNG SHING TEMPLE
5. CHEUNG CHUN YUEN CLAN HALL
6. TANG CHING LOK CLAN HALL
7. BANYAN TREE HOUSE
8. TANG CHAN YUI KUEN CLAN HALL
9. PING MO BRIDGE
10. CHOU WONG YI KUNG STUDY HALL

Tin Hau Temple

7

6

5

4

3

Shui Mei Tsuen

8

9

Shui Tau Tsuen

10

1

2

to KAM TIN ROAD

To KAT HING WAI

← to YUEN LONG

to SHEK KONG →

quashed in 1899. They were finally returned to the villagers in 1925 through the personal efforts of the then governor, Sir Reginald Stubbs.

On leaving the walled village, continue a short way down the Kam Tin Road towards Yuen Long until, just short of the traffic lights, you will find a turning to the right with a school on the corner. This narrow lane is the only approach to Shui Tau Tsuen and Shui Mei Tsuen which together offer a concentration of monuments and buildings that can be found nowhere else in the territory. The twisting road is only one lane wide and it takes patience and courtesy on all sides to negotiate it. One reason for the reluctance of the locals to open their

village to a second heritage trail is their very valid fear concerning the extra traffic. Motorists are also asked to be considerate when parking. Since the distance from Kat Hing Wai is only about a kilometre it is easy to walk.

After crossing the bridge over the narrow river, take the second left-hand fork at the beginning of the village. You will find yourself almost immediately between two study halls. On the left is the **Yi Tai study hall** which is open to the public at weekends and on Public Holidays. Yi Tai ('Two Immortals') study hall was built by a local learned society of sixteen scholar gentry not only as a study hall but also as a resting place for the two immortals whose home on the same site in a *fung shui*

Yi Tai study hall on the right with So Lau Yuen study hall opposite

Inside So Lau Yuen study hall

pagoda had been demolished. These immortals, Man Cheong and Kwan Ti, can be seen on the left as you enter the hall flanked by the God of Wealth on the left and the City God on the right. These statues are replicas: the ancient originals were stolen in 1978.

The building is entered by a lane of fine white stones so those studying there were always known as the 'White Stone Lane Scholars'. The layout is typical of a study hall with side rooms that could be screened off and upstairs rooms at each corner where teacher and students slept. Before you leave note the fine painted pierced wood screens and the decorative grills instead of windows. If you stand with your back to the altar, the

pierced wood carving above the right-hand corner room contains the following three characters: *fuk* on the left, *luk* in the centre, and *sau* on the right, after the three star gods of happiness, wealth, and long life.

On the opposite side of the road is **So Lau Yuen study hall**. So Lau Yuen literally means, 'place for swimming uphill and reaching one's goal' (see page 32). The great stone over the entrance gate was written by a well known Tang calligrapher, Tang Ying Yuen (b. 1755).

Cross the square the other side of the study halls, passing the **Earth God Shrine** on your right, and continue about 100 metres down the left-hand path, past an old village well complete with mechanical pump. You will come out into a forecourt of another fine building recently renovated with the help of the Antiquities and Monuments Office. This is the **Loi Shing Tong**, an

The Chinese characters, fuk, luk, *and* sau *in the Yi Tai study hall*

100

Cheung Chun Yuen ancestral hall

little is **Cheung Chun Yuen**, an ancestral hall and former martial arts school, probably built in the 1870s. It has its own parade ground on the right-hand side. Inside the building are three great antique iron spears, the heaviest of which weighs 112 catties. The altar is distinguished by a beautiful old set of altar vessels inlaid with enamel and two fine portraits of the founding ancestors of this branch of the Tang clan. The two large enclosed areas beside the clan hall were used for martial arts training.

As you come out of Cheung Chun Yuen, the wall of the **Tang Ching Lok ancestral hall** will be on your right. Follow this wall to the far corner ahead of you, then turn right to enter the forecourt. This magnificent three-hall clan hall was probably built in the late eighteenth century and you can count yourself very lucky if you find it open to visitors. It is still used in the traditional way for holding festivities, ceremonies, or meetings of the clan elders.

After admiring the hall with its great Shekwan pottery dragon fish on the roof ridges, continue along the path until it bends to the right, then take the first path to the left. It will bring you to a sight you must not miss. This magnificent *fung shui* **banyan tree** is more than four hundred years old. The

ancestral hall erected in 1701. Notice the elegant fleur-de-lis pattern of the plaster work on each side under the eaves. The interior is very attractive with colourful carved and painted motifs. Lying outside the hall against a wall as you enter the forecourt is an old quern stone (see page 9).

Next to the Loi Shing Tong, you will find a well-maintained, modern **Hung Shing Temple** (see page 78) usually kept closed off with an iron grill, perhaps installed as a result of the thefts from the Yi Tai study hall in in 1978. The furnishings and statues inside the temple are the original ones preserved from the previous temple. Notice the intricate embroidery of the ceiling hangings of the altar on the left.

Beyond the temple and set back a

house that has been engulfed amid the twisting roots of the tree is said to date to pre-clearance days, that is before 1662 (see page 4). If its flourishing appearance is anything to go by, Kam Tin is set to continue on its present prosperous course.

Continue along the path round to the right and down to the road. Turn right on to the road and walk along, passing, on the right, the back of the Tang Chan Yui Kuen ancestral hall. The length of its name is due to the fact that it was built in honour of three brothers all of whose names are included. The hall was built around 1770, but sadly, during its 1977 restoration, the original carved beams were replaced by concrete. This hall is usually kept locked.

Banyan tree and remains of old house

Another 100 metres along you will find a tree with a small tree shrine on the left-hand side of the road. Take the path just beyond it to the left, turning right as soon as you can to cross the river. The **Ping Mo Bridge** over the river tells a tale of filial piety. Tang Tsuen Yuen faithfully carried his

Ping Mo Bridge

mother on his back twice a day over the river on her visits to the family. Meanwhile he saved every cent he could spare to build a bridge for her convenience (and perhaps his too!). After many years of saving, the bridge was finally built in 1710. A stone plaque records this filial deed and the

OPENING HOURS of Yi Tai study hall

9 a.m. to 1 p.m. and 2 p.m. to 5 p.m:
Saturdays, Sundays and Public Holidays
Closed: first three days of Chinese New Year

name of the bridge, which is, of course, 'Bridge for the Convenience of the Mother'.

Finally, on the other side of the bridge is the **Chou Wong Yi Kung study hall** erected in 1683 to commemorate the two Mandarins who finally persuaded the emperor to repeal the evacuation order and allow the people to return to their homes (see page 4). This hall is kept locked except at times of the *Dajiao* (see page 39) when it becomes the focus of activity. A story is told that during the Japanese occupation the Tang elders decided to postpone the ten-yearly festival.

However on the appropriate day a troupe of opera singers appeared in the village to the amazement of the villagers. The leader of the troupe claimed that he had been hired by two old men and when he was shown the portraits of Chou and Wong he immediately recognized them as the old men who had hired him. And so the festival went ahead as usual.

This brings you to the end of the tour. If you go back to the road and continue along it you will arrive back at the fork where the walk began.

PUBLIC TRANSPORT

KMB

64K	Yuen Long West to Tai Po KCR station
51	Tsuen Wan ferry to Kam Tin
54	Yuen Long West to Sheung Tsuen (Shek Kong) via Kam Tin Road

PUBLIC LIGHT BUS (Green)

601	Fung Cheung Street, Yuen Long to Pak Wai Tsuen, Kam Tin (this takes you right up to the Kam Tin trail villages)
602	Fung Cheung Street, Yuen Long to Tai Kong Po via Kam Tin Road
71	Tai Hang Street, Yuen Long to Shek Wu Tong (Ho Pui) via Kam Tin Road
72	Tai Hang Street, Yuen Long to Lui Kung Tin via Kam Tin Road

CHAPTER 3

SAN TIN

San Tin is easily accessible by car and can be combined with a visit, to the Lok Ma Chau Lookout Post (No. 7 on the north-west New Territories Countryside Series map) if you wish to get a view of China across the river and fast-diminishing fish ponds. It is easy to find your way around San Tin and does not involve too much walking. In a short half-day tour, you can get a real feel of the warmth and friendliness of a clan village.

If travelling by car along the motorway from Fanling to Yuen Long, exit at Pak Shek Au, and, after continuing for about a mile parallel to the motorway, the road crosses the dual carriageway and joins the old Castle Peak Road. The best access to San Tin is provided by taking the first, very narrow lane to the right, signposted to **Fan Tin Tsuen**, almost immediately after passing the playing field opposite the Esso service station.

If you are coming from Yuen Long, leave the motorway at Mai Po, turning right on to the old Castle Peak Road, and follow the signs to San Tin, taking the third narrow lane to the left. This lane will lead you down into the village past the fine pink **Earth God Shrine** on your right. You can park along this lane, or

Earth God Shrine

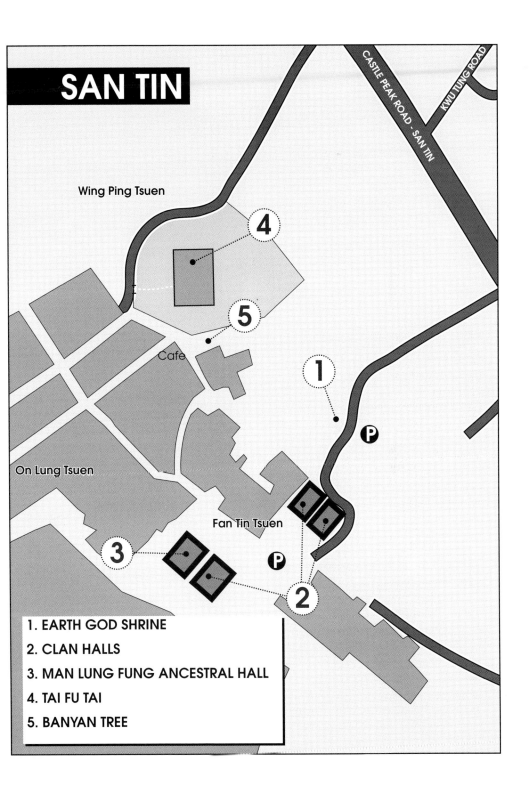

SAN TIN

Wing Ping Tsuen

④

⑤

Cafe

①

On Lung Tsuen

Fan Tin Tsuen

③

②

CASTLE PEAK ROAD - SAN TIN

KWU TUNG ROAD

1. EARTH GOD SHRINE

2. CLAN HALLS

3. MAN LUNG FUNG ANCESTRAL HALL

4. TAI FU TAI

5. BANYAN TREE

continue into the village and park in the square.

San Tin is the heartlands of the Man clan who settled the area in the fifteenth century. Being the last clan to arrive, by this time the better land had already been taken by other clans, such as the Tangs, and so the Mans had to make the best of the low-lying marshy ground that was left. You will see four clan halls around the square in Fan Tin Tsuen, one of mini villages that together make up San Tin. But only the **Man Lung Fung ancestral hall** is open to the public and it is signposted.

The Man Lung Fung clan hall backs on to the far left-hand side of the square, and faces north. If you take the lane alongside its west wall, you will come to the front of the hall looking out over a spacious courtyard to the fields and fishponds beyond. The hall is believed to have been built in the mid-seventeenth century. Inside, the first hall is called the To Shu Tong or 'Speaking with Scholarship' Hall. Perhaps it was formerly used as a study hall. This hall is unusual in that the spirit tablets are housed, not at the very back, but instead on an altar in the centre of the hall. Notice the grand stone columns and the massive arrangement of beams supporting the roofs. The supporting brackets are finely carved and painted.

As you leave the hall, make your way round to the back again, passing through the small, leafy sitting-out area. Turn left and take the left-hand path into the village. At the small

Man Lung Fung ancestral hall

crossroads, keep straight on, veering slightly to the right. You will pass some village shops and interesting old houses as well as other lanes just asking to be explored. After five minutes or so the houses end. Turn right and you should come out by the wall of the grounds of the Tai Fu Tai. The entrance is a few steps to the left.

The **Tai Fu Tai** (No. 8 on the north-west New Territories Countryside Series map) is the only remaining Mandarin's house in Hong Kong. It has been restored to its original grandeur and is open to the public. It was propably built in 1865 by Man Cheung Long whose portrait together with that of his wife graces the central hall. Man Cheung Long was a member of the twenty-first generation of Mans and very successful in business. Because of his good works, he had the title of Tai Fu (Great Man) bestowed on him by the reigning Qing Emperor.

Notice the outside of the house with its symmetry: the three entrances are evenly spaced along the front and there are no windows. The boat-shaped roof ridge has detailed mouldings at each end and the centre is filled with Shekwan pottery figurines in the niches. There is also a fine frieze of Shekwan pottery figurines each side of the main door under the eaves, but sadly many of the little people have lost their heads.

Screen doors, Tai Fu Tai

As you go inside, you will pass doorways on both sides with painted glass panels and the moulded swags of leaves and flowers in the Victorian classical style, showing Western influences. Look carefully at the green and gold carvings on the doors of the screens that separate off the side rooms. You will find auspicious symbols, including vases, symbolizing peace, with playful lions each side and many different sorts of flowers, fruits and leaves (see page 20). The decorative wooden surrounds of the main hall, and the carving on the upper balcony are also worth careful examination. In the main hall under the eaves, are two honorific boards addressed to the parents and grandparents of Man Cheung Long. These boards are unique in Hong Kong in that the Manchu calligraphy of the Qing Dynasty hangs on one side, with traditional Chinese calligraphy on the other.

If you turn to the left at the end of the main hall, you will find yourself in a scholar's studio with its own enclosed courtyard. Notice the moulding of the resolute carp swimming upstream (see page 32) and the elegant calligraphy on either side of the tile-filled window. (If you wish to see how the studio of a scholar of the last century would have been furnished, you should visit the Tsui Gallery on the eleventh floor of the old China Bank Building in Queen's Road, Central.)

At the other side of the main hall, you will find the kitchens with a row of holes designed to fit the clay cooking pots on one side and, on the other, two much larger holes to accommodate the woks that you can still see in place. In the passage between the main hall and the kitchens is a great hollowed-out log lying on the floor. This is a peanut press designed to extract peanut oil for cooking. A small piece of machinery was placed at one end which crushed the peanuts, depositing the flesh into the hollowed-out log. The oil gravitated to the top and flowed out of a hole at the other end of the log.

At the back of this passage are the storerooms and a row of wooden lavatories. The garden behind the house, which is no longer open to the public, used to have a fine lychee orchard.

On leaving the house, if you turn left there is a noodle and drinks shop on the opposite side of the road where you can sit outside and take a break. Notice the fine old **banyan tree** to the right of the shop with the incense sticks, showing evidence of the respect which it is accorded. Make your way back to the car by the same route, or, if you feel like exploring, pick an alternative lane on the right. There are many peaceful corners, and interesting old houses that make walking in San Tin, in almost any direction, worthwhile and enjoyable.

OPENING HOURS of the Tai Fu Tai

9 a.m. to 1 p.m. and 2 p.m. to 5 p.m.
Closed: Tuesdays, Christmas Day, Boxing Day, New Year's Day, and the first three days of Lunar New Year

PUBLIC TRANSPORT	
KMB	
76K	Yuen Long West to Wah Ming via Castle Peak Road
73K	Sheung Shui to Man Kam To
PUBLIC LIGHT BUS (Green)	
75	Fook Hong Street, Yuen Long to Ha Wan Tsuen via Castle Peak Road
76	Fook Hong Street, Yuen Long to Siu Hom Tsuen

ADDITIONAL PLACES OF INTEREST ALONG CASTLE PEAK ROAD

East of San Tin there are two places off Castle Peak Road which are well worth a visit.

1. Ho Sheung Heung

Ho Sheung Heung is typical of the thrill of venturing into what feels like the back of beyond to be rewarded by finding not just one, but two special sights. Turn left as you leave San Tin on to Castle Peak Road, heading towards Fanling. After about three kilometres turn left at the signpost to Ho Sheung Heung. Continue for about a mile along this rather winding road

Tin Hau Temple, Ho Sheung Heung

until you take a rather unexpected turn to the right that is signposted only in Chinese characters. Another mile or so down this road, you round a corner and there nestling snugly in the bend of the road, with its *fung shui* woods behind it, is a gem of a **Tin Hau temple** with three entrances. This is a temple to wander round and savour on your own. Notice among other things, the temple kitchen in the centre with its shrine to the Kitchen God. The main hall on the left is dedicated to Tin Hau (see page 76) whereas the right-hand hall is given over to the worship of Buddha. This is a good example of the way popular religion encompasses both Taoism and Buddhism.

After leaving, continue down the road, through the village of Ho Sheung Heung, until you come to a small square, where you should be able to park. On the left-hand side of the square as you enter, you will see the **Hau Kui Shek Tong**. The Hau is one of the five great clans of the New Territories (see page 38), being only the second clan to settle here as far back as the twelfth century. This clan hall was built in the middle of the eighteenth century and has recently been restored and opened to the public. It has three halls and two courtyards. Notice the intricately carved roof brackets with their small, but lively and attractive, brightly painted scenes from Chinese

PUBLIC TRANSPORT	
Public Light Bus (Green)	
51K	Sheung Shui KCR station to Ho Sheung Heung

history and mythology. In front of you as you enter and cross the first courtyard under the eaves of the second roof, there is a delightful character in yellow with a definite paunch and a black top hat accompanied by his elephant. He is paired with a man and his rhinoceros on the right.

2. *Tsung Pak Long*

Turn left as you leave San Tin on to Castle Peak Road, heading towards Fanling. After about four kilometres turn left at the signpost to Tsung Pak Long, driving into this multi-clan village. Each clan here has its own clan hall, and, on the northern side of the village, you can find five clan halls in a row, all exactly the same size and shape so that no single clan can feel any loss of face.

But the architectural gem of this village is the walled compound called **Hakka Wai**, which is on the south-eastern side of the village. Inside, the double row of identical houses, built between 1904 and 1905, is extremely secure with a wall completely enclosing them and a three-storey watchtower. Even today, it is difficult to gain access through the locked entrance and depends on the kindness of a local inhabitant. The village is in excellent condition and remains exactly as it was when it was built, with no modern three-storey villas replacing the old houses. The entrance is guarded by a white *fung shui* wall on either side. Inside, in the centre of the front row of houses, there is a small, but richly decorated ancestor hall. The houses themselves are very attractive with delicate murals, plaster mouldings, and realistic gargoyles in the shape of frogs, fishes, and bats. This village community gives an impression of peace, security, and belonging that some people might feel envious of.

PUBLIC TRANSPORT

Public Light Bus (Green)

50K	Sheung Shui KCR station to Hang Tau
51K	Sheung Shui KCR station to Ho Sheung Heung

CHAPTER 4

SHEUNG SHUI

The pride of Sheung Shui is the Liu Man Shek Tong Clan Hall (No. 9 on the north-west New Territories Countryside Series map). If you are coming by car from Fanling, it is easier to find the way if you ignore the Sheung Shui exit from the Fanling–Yuen Long Highway, and turn off at the next one, signposted (on a yellow sign) to Man Kam To. Take the third turning off the roundabout on to Po Shek Wu Road. If you are coming from Yuen Long take the turning off the motorway that is signposted to Sheung Shui and Man Kam To. From either direction, you will then cross over the first set of traffic lights and the KCR line and, at the next set of lights, turn left down Po Wan Road. If you then take the first turning to the right, it will lead you to a convenient parking area at the edge of Sheung Shui Wai. A narrow road from the far corner of this car park leads into Sheung Shui—a two-minute walk.

If you come by KCR to Sheung Shui Station, you will have a ten-minute walk to Sheung Shui Wai (or you can either take a taxi straight to the Liu Man Shek Tong clan hall). From Po Shek Wu Road, turn left at the first major crossroads with traffic lights into Po Wan Road and then cut down on to the car park road on your right. Follow the road past the first car park and into the second one, then take the narrow road into Sheung Shui.

On the way into the village you will pass several very fine *fung shui* trees, some with their roots encased in gigantic pink concrete pots. Once in the square, take a look to your left. You will see the gatehouse of **Wai Loi Tsuen walled village**, the oldest part of Sheung Shui. Its lower half is built of reddish stone denoting both wealth and good luck—wealth because the prized red stone had to be brought

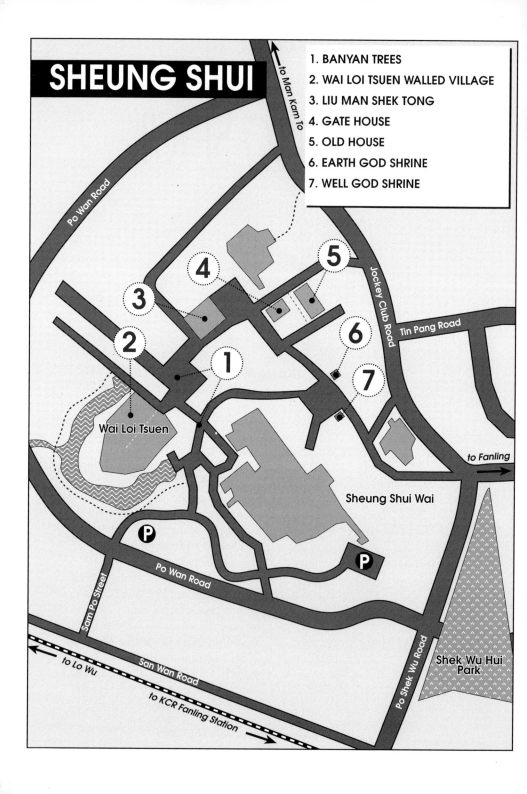

Entrance to Wai Lo Tsuen

from distant quarries and cost much more than local stone. The Liu clan came originally from Fujian during the Yuan Dynasty (1271–1368) but did not settle in Wai Lo Tsuen until the end of the sixteenth century. At that time, two *fung shui* experts of the seventh and eighth generations decided to unify the clan and carefully chose an auspicious site. They clearly chose well because not only did the clan multiply and spread, founding the other villages that make up the present Sheung Shui, but they also became wealthy and influential. In the genealogy of the Liu clan, no fewer than forty-seven clan members passed the Imperial Civil Service Examination—a great achievement for such a small place. This walled village is one of the few to

have retained its original moat on three sides. The wall and the moat were constructed between 1646 and 1647. You can walk around the village, catching glimpses of the remaining walls. The old covered well is at the far right-hand corner as you enter.

As you come out of the walled village, cross the square and take the narrow footpath on the left. The fine roof ridge of the **Liu Man Shek Tong** is quite unmistakable, but you cannot see the clan hall itself from the main path since it is hidden behind its 'spirit wall', the first line of defence against evil spirits. The name 'Man Shek' means '10,000 Shi', a Shi being a measured unit of grain a year. It is so called because a remote ancestor, Liu Kong, and his four sons, living in the Song Dynasty (960–1279) were, all five, high government officials, each one earning 2,000 Shi of grain, making a grand total of 10,000 Shi.

This clan hall was built in 1751. It was used as a school for approximately fifty years up to 1980, but was restored to its original design in 1985. It is said to possess some of the richest wood carvings of all the clan halls in the New Territories. Before you go into the hall, notice the stone columns and finely carved wooden brackets supporting the roof. You should also take a look at the wooden fascia board running right across the front of the hall above the guardian lions. The frieze shows a wealth of auspicious plants, flowers, mythical animals, and legendary figures.

The inscription confers peace on the house and the people who live there

The Liu Man Shek Tong consists of three halls separated by two spacious courtyards. The three altars for the spirit tablets are against the back wall of the furthest hall. As you make your way in, notice the finely carved roof beams. Round the walls of the hall are murals, many of which evoke the mountain scenery beloved of the Taoists. Finally, before you leave, take a look at the brightly coloured, moulded plaster decorations both inside and outside the hall which portray very typical symbolic Chinese motives.

As you leave the hall, turn left and follow the narrow lane at the side of the clan hall. At the back of the hall is an open courtyard with an exit on its right. Once on the next path, you will see, on the corner in front of you, the gatehouse of a traditional **old house**

with *wok-yee* gables. Further along the path by the side of the house is a doorway over which hangs a fine stucco panel with calligraphy (in the picture above). The *wok-yee* gables are so called because they are shaped like the handles of a wok. It is said that only a scholar was allowed to own a house with gables shaped like these.

Retrace your steps and take the path through the courtyard (in the picture opposite) and on through the village. After a few minutes you will reach another square. An altar to the local **Earth God** stands on your left as you enter it, with a smart offering table in front of it. On the opposite side of the square, in front of a shop, is the old village well, with its mouth covered and securely locked. It is surrounded by a low wall with a niche built into the

114

Path through the courtyard

far side for the **Well God Shrine**, which is generally bristling with incense sticks and candles.

Walk back towards Wai Loi Tsuen taking the wider road with the playground on its left-hand side. Once back at the walled village take the narrow path to the right of the gatehouse. You can walk all the way around the moat, observing the remaining village walls, before arriving back at the car park.

OPENING HOURS of Liu Man Shek Tong

9 a.m. to 1 p.m. and 2 p.m. to 5 p.m: Wednesdays, Thursdays, Saturdays, Sundays, and Public Holidays
Closed: Mondays, Tuesdays, and Fridays

PUBLIC TRANSPORT	
KMB	
70	Jordon ferry pier, Kowloon to Sheung Shui
70X	Kwun Tong to Sheung Shui
PUBLIC LIGHT BUS (Green)	
57K	Sheung Shui KCR station to Tong Kung Leng via Po Shek Wu Road
58K	Sheung Shui KCR station to Ping Kong via Po Shek Wu Road

N.B. It takes between ten and fifteen minutes to walk from the Bus Terminus or from the KCR Railway Station.

CHAPTER 5

THE FANLING AREA

If you come by train to Fanling, you'll have a pleasant ten- to fifteen-minute walk to **Fan Ling Wai**. Walk straight out of the station until you come to a roundabout, then turn left into San Wan Road, walking along the side of the railway line for about five minutes. The third turning on the right, opposite the Fanling swimming pool, will take you into Fan Ling Wai. Drivers can reach Fan Ling Wai the same way, driving along the San Wan Road in the direction of Sheung Shui, and turning right into Fan Ling Wai. An alternative is from Jockey Club Road, driving towards Sheung Shui, and entering Fan Ling Wai from the north. After crossing straight over the roundabout (with the magistracy on its left) take the second turning left between a China Light substation and some modern pink and white villas. It is easier to park if you arrive from this direction.

Having entered the village from San Wan Road, follow the main path through the centre. You will pass a cream painted clan hall on your right, then the path widens into a village square with a banyan tree and a tree shrine on the left. Follow the path as it bends to the left. You will come out into a large square with the walled village of Fan Ling Wai on the left and a large pond in front of it. This village is the heartland of the Pang clan, one of the five great clans of the New Territories. They are said to have arrived from Guangxi province late in the Song Dynasty and settled in the Fanling area between 1120 and 1280. Fan Ling Wai has an attractive entrance looking out over its man-made *fung shui* pond and guarded by two canons, one large and one small. The impressive walls boast three watchtowers and the red sandstone surrounds to the door denote the wealth of the Pangs. Over

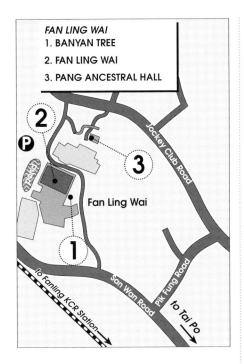

FAN LING WAI
1. BANYAN TREE
2. FAN LING WAI
3. PANG ANCESTRAL HALL

Fan Ling Wai

home there. You will be very lucky if you manage to gain access to the Pang hall since it is generally kept locked, but it has fine decoration and carvings and murals inside.

The other old and interesting part of Fan Ling is about two and a half miles from Fanling Station, but can be reached by the Green Minibus No. 54K.

If you are travelling by car, make your way back to the roundabout with the Fanling Magistracy standing among its palm trees on one side. Take the Sha Tau Kok Road and then the first turning to the right on to Lok Yip Street. Now look for the third turning to the left (On Chuen Street) which can be identified by the array of village signposts. Next take the first right on to Lok Tung Street, drive over a bridge and then turn left. Now follow the narrow concrete road. It may be small and feel as if it cannot possibly lead anywhere, but be patient. You will eventually pass two walled villages.

the gateway and below each of the gun ports you will see an elegant triangle of three white circles. Some say that these circles denote the trinity of Heaven, earth, and man, with the white colour reflecting the void at the centre of the universe (see page 59).

Return to the main path through the village and continue along it. You will see the **Pang ancestral hall** on the right, in its own square set back from the road. It was built in about 1884 and has two chambers and one courtyard. Clan halls were traditionally built on neutral ground outside the villages so that residents of any of the cluster of villages would feel equally at

Entrance to Ma Wat Wai

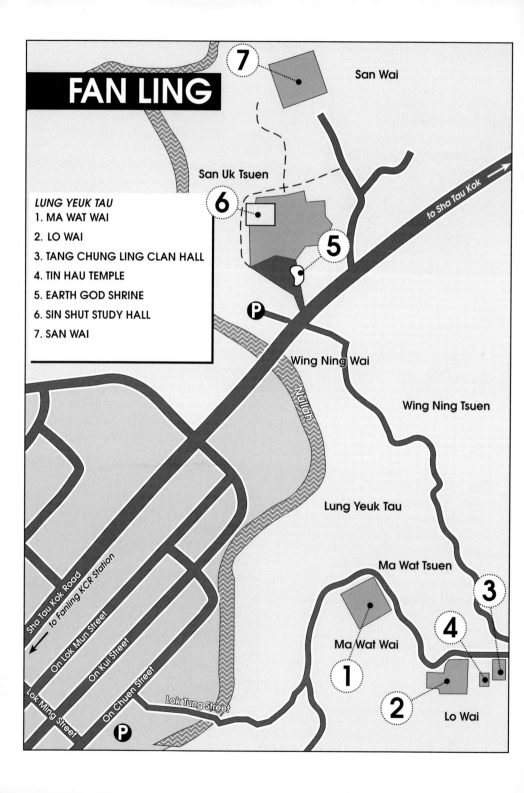

FAN LING

LUNG YEUK TAU
1. MA WAT WAI
2. LO WAI
3. TANG CHUNG LING CLAN HALL
4. TIN HAU TEMPLE
5. EARTH GOD SHRINE
6. SIN SHUT STUDY HALL
7. SAN WAI

San Wai

San Uk Tsuen

to Sha Tau Kok

Wing Ning Wai

Wing Ning Tsuen

Nullah

Lung Yeuk Tau

Ma Wat Tsuen

Ma Wat Wai

Lo Wai

Sha Tau Kok Road
to Fanling KCR Station

On Lok Mun Street

On Kui Street

On Chuen Street

Lok Ming Street

Lok Tung Street

The first, **Ma Wat Wai**, has an excellent pair of cast-iron gates. The second is **Lo Wai** which is the oldest walled village in the area and was declared a public monument in 1997. Lo Wai must be entered at an angle. This makes it easy for humans to gain entrance while thwarting evil spirits who only travel in straight lines. The villages in this area are part of the Tang clan's domains. Members of the clan moved here from the main Tang settlement at Kam Tin in the thirteenth century. The locality in all comprises eleven villages and is known as **Lung Yeuk Tau**.

A few houses beyond Lo Wai, you will come to a square where you can park the car. The large **Tang Chung Ling ancestral hall** was built in the early sixteenth century and serves the whole of the Lung Yeuk Tau area. It was most recently used as a school. It may be locked, but the local villagers are usually very obliging and kind about finding keys and letting one in. It is one of the largest clan halls in the New Territories and its peaceful rural setting, with its back to the hills, makes it particularly attractive. Notice the wooden beams and bracket supports to the roof which are intricately carved with a series of vivid dragon fish swimming their way up towards the apex.

The rear hall houses the three altars with the central altar for the founding ancestors including the Song princess and her husband, Tang Wai Kip (see page 38). You can distinguish these soul

tablets by their more elaborate surrounds carved with dragon heads. The altar on the left is dedicated to clan members who achieved high ranks in the imperial court or made special contributions to the clan. The right-hand altar is dedicated to righteous members of the clan. Among these soul tablets is one to 'the righteous servant' Tang Si Meng. Towards the end of the sixteenth century, he and his master were kidnapped for ransom. The brave servant passed himself off as his master's son and persuaded the kidnappers to let his master go free in order to raise the ransom. As soon as his master was safely away, Tang Si Meng drowned himself in the sea, thus saving his master's life and fortune.

Before you leave, look also at the finely carved and painted surrounds to the altars and particularly the moulded plaster pictures at the lower corners with their delightful vignettes of

Plaster figures, Tang Chung Ling clan hall

ancient China with mandarins in session, on their travels, and at leisure.

The small temple to the right of the hall is dedicated to **Tin Hau**, Goddess of the Sea (see page 76). It is said by the village elders to be even older than the clan hall. The friezes on either side of the door under the eaves are worth looking at carefully with their scenes of mountains, rivers, bridges, and a walled city complete with watchman. When you go inside try to get a peep at the front of the altar table which is finely carved. You will have to bend down and peer between the legs of the table in front of it. Tin Hau, on the main altar, is flanked by her two guardians, Thousand *Li* Eye and Favourable Wind Ear. The two bells in the left chamber were cast in 1695 and 1700 respectively, the larger one weighing 110 kilograms.

If you take the even narrower road to the left, opposite the ancestral hall, it will wind its way past three small villages on the left-hand side, finally coming out on to

Sin Shut Study Hall

the Sha Tau Kok Road. Cross the main road and park the car in the small lane on the left. You are now on the edge of the village of San Uk Tsuen and you can see the other sights on foot.

However, if you prefer not to walk, turn right into Sha Tau Kok Road then take the first small road to the left, signposted to Kan Lung Wai. This lane will bring you round to the front of the walled village known now as San Wai.

If you walk, you will find yourself in a square with an **Earth God Shrine** on the right. Take the path at the far left-hand corner of the square by the village shop. Pass this and another small shop on the right, and continue alongside a row of typical village houses with a concreted area in front for drying the rice.

Favourable Wind Ear

Thousand Li *Eye*

120

There is a good example of an old quern stone lying out on the concrete here (see page 9). Half way along the row of houses and set a little back in a compound is the **Sin Shut Study Hall**, built in 1840 and now used as an ancestor hall. You will be very lucky if you get inside to see it. The key gets passed in rotation among the Tang villagers and no one ever knows who actually has the key on any given day. The terracotta decorations under the eaves on either side of the main door are almost lace-like in their delicacy. Inside there are some fine old carvings.

If you turn right at the first possible turning after the hall, and then turn left on to the first footpath, after about three minutes, you will reach a square with the walled village of **San Wai** (Kan Lung Wai) on its right. The walls have recently been restored and are perhaps the most complete in the territory. The gatehouse is without a doubt the finest and very unusual in that it has a double structure with an inner and an outer hall. The two characters carved over the gateway are Kun Lung, which gave the village its original name. The tower is surmounted by a fine, decorated boat-shaped ridge.

Inside the village, more and more houses are being replaced by modern, three-storey villas. But to the left of the entrance is a very fine classic village house with a swallow's-tail roof ridge. A spirit wall runs in front of it. Notice the decorated panels over the doors and the general lack of windows. A small ancestor shrine stands at the end of the main path.

PUBLIC TRANSPORT	
KMB	
78K	Sheung Shui KCR station to Sha Tau Kok (along Sha Tau Kok Road)
PUBLIC LIGHT BUS (Green)	
52K	Fanling KCR station to Ping Che via Lung Yeuk Tau
53K	Fan Ling Wai to Luen Wo Hui via Fanling KCR station
54K	Fanling KCR station to Lung Yeuk Tau (circular), passing Lo Wai and Tsz Tong Tsuen
55K	Sheung Shui KCR station to Sha Tau Kok

ADDITIONAL PLACES OF INTEREST ALONG THE SHA TAU KOK ROAD

The Kan Yung Shu Uk study hall and the Cheung Shan Temple are linked by their history, and are to be found not far from each other on either side of the Sha Tau Kok Road north of Fanling.

1. Sheung Wo Hang and Kan Yung Shu Uk

About six kilometres north of Fanling, just before the Sha Tau Kok Road bends to the left, turn right at the signpost to Sheung Wo Hang. The narrow road disappears down a leafy glade. Wo Hang means 'Valley of Rice'. It was settled by the Li clan who were Hakka people, in about 1710, and is still, together with its sister villages of Ha Wo Hang and Wo Hang Tai, mainly inhabited by the descendants of its founders.

There is limited parking down the lane by the village and it may be better to park in a layby on the main road and walk. This peaceful, small community contains a very imposing study hall that continued to operate as a primary school right up to 1986. It has since been restored by the Antiquities and Monuments Office and is open to the public. Walk up the hill along the concrete path towards the village. Then turn right and continue along the path with the children's playground on the right. The Kan Yung Shu Uk is signposted. The path passes just below the concrete rice-drying terraces of a row of village houses before entering an ancient *fung shui* wood. Continue on to the very end of the path, keeping left and uphill. You will arrive at the grey brick study hall.

The characters over the door give the name, **Kan Yung Shu Uk**, literally, 'Mirror Hibiscus Study Hall'. The name may refer to a Tang legend about Li Gu Yan, who failed the Imperial Civil Service Exam. He then happened to meet an old Sichuan woman who predicted that he would pass the exam under a hibiscus-shaped mirror. He pondered deeply on the meaning of her words, but all became clear when he next presented himself as a candidate and was asked to write a poem entitled, 'The Hibiscus-shaped Mirror'. Li Gu Yuan not only passed the exam, but went on to become a prime minister.

The study hall was named in 1872 by a well-known local scholar, Li Pui Yuen, who also wrote the couplets on either side of the Cheung Shan Temple. Li Pui Yuen became famous when one of his students achieved the distinction of coming first in one of the Imperial civil service examinations. It was the first time anyone from the area had passed that examination for over two hundred years. The name, Kang Yung may also refer to the successful student who was called Tang Yung Kang.

The interior of the hall is simple and functional. Some of the desks and uncomfortable-looking benches are still in place. The teacher and the students from further away would have slept in the lofts at each corner. The peaceful outlook and quiet position seem very conducive to scholarship.

2. Cheung Shan Temple

About five kilometres north of Fanling along the Sha Tau Kok Road (a little before you reach the turning for Sheung Wo Hang), turn right on to Wo Keng Shan Road, a wide new road that is at present signposted to a landfill. About one and a half kilometres up this road you will find a temple on the right. It is at present dangerously dilapidated and is kept shut, but is scheduled for renovation by the Antiquities and Monuments Office. This temple is one of the oldest Buddhist nunneries in the territory, probably founded in the late eighteenth century as a refuge and resting place for travellers crossing the wild and dangerous pass on their way to Shenzhen. Tigers were a serious problem in the area. The nuns dispensed tea to any traveller, and many cups must have been consumed if the government surveys of 1904 and 1906 are correct that 20,000 people a month used the road, carrying about 400 tonnes of goods.

Over the door of the temple is a couplet written by Li Pui Yuen, the teacher from Sheung Wo Hang who retired to this nunnery in his old age. The right-hand couplet has been translated by Dr P. Hase as follows:-

> Friends part reluctantly at the Pavilion of Separation by the ancient road. There they think of the parting of their ways.
>
> They shelter from rain and get protection from dust. Their needs are met day after day.

This is matched by the left-hand couplet which says:-

> On the mountain the birds greet the spring while the monastery proclaims the dawn of all things.
>
> The scent of incense on the breeze, and the sound of the bell fulfil my needs year after year.

The bell alluded to was donated by the local villages in 1789.

After the spectacular success of Li Pui Yuen's pupil, Tang Yung Kang, which he ascribed to his night at the temple and the encouragement of his old teacher before setting out, it became a tradition for all students from the study hall at Sheung Wo Hang to spend their first night at this temple before travelling on to Guangdong to sit for the Provincial Examination.

Cheung Shan Temple

CHAPTER 6

SHA TIN

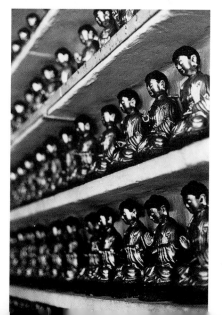

Because of the parking problems, it is simpler to use public transport when visiting Sha Tin. The three places suggested here are quite far apart, but the **Ten Thousand Buddha Temple** makes an enjoyable half-day outing on its own. There about two hundred and fifty steps to climb to reach the temple. Make sure you take some water, especially in summer.

Leave Sha Tin KCR Station by the ramp on the left signposted 'taxis and pedestrians'. On the wall, you will see the first of the yellow signs to the temple. Coming down the ramp you will see interesting old village houses on the left, and at the bottom is a useful mapboard. If you follow the main road, then take the first turning to the left on to Pai Tau Street, you will arrive at a large new Buddhist temple complex with its own tram lift on the right-hand side to carry worshippers to the top. Do not be misled into thinking that this is your destination. The path to the Ten Thousand Buddha Temple passes alongside the car park at the right of this complex and is marked with small yellow signposts. It enters the woodland, wanders between some

Buddhas in the Ten Thousand Buddha Temple

124

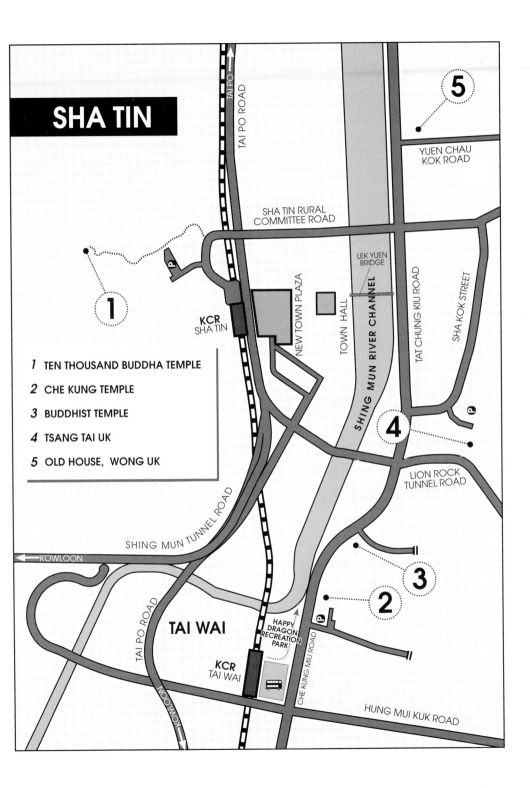

SHA TIN

5

YUEN CHAU KOK ROAD

TAI PO ROAD

TAI PO

SHA TIN RURAL COMMITTEE ROAD

LEK YUEN BRIDGE

TAT CHUNG KIU ROAD

SHA KOK STREET

1

P

NEW TOWN PLAZA

TOWN HALL

SHING MUN RIVER CHANNEL

KCR SHA TIN

1 TEN THOUSAND BUDDHA TEMPLE

2 CHE KUNG TEMPLE

3 BUDDHIST TEMPLE

4 TSANG TAI UK

5 OLD HOUSE, WONG UK

4

P

LION ROCK TUNNEL ROAD

SHING MUN TUNNEL ROAD

KOWLOON

3

2

TAI PO ROAD

TAI WAI

P

HAPPY DRAGON RECREATION PARK

CHE KUNG MIU ROAD

KCR TAI WAI

KOWLOON

HUNG MUI KUK ROAD

stalls selling drinks and incense, and then starts to climb. The route will probably take you under half an hour depending on your speed of ascent, and you will eventually emerge beside the main temple hall.

The walls of the main hall are lined, so it is said, with twelve thousand eight hundred Buddhas. Each is slightly different in posture or gesture, and they represent actual Buddhas. They were donated by worshippers and made individually of local clay by twelve craftsmen from Shanghai who worked in the temple for ten years to complete them. On the lowest level they are

Pagoda

guarded by eighty-four representatives from Lord Buddha's army. The approach to the temple is guarded by two rows of Lohans and two Bodhisattvas, Wen Shu on a lion and Pu

Xian on an elephant (see page 72). Between them is the statue of Wei To facing into the main hall on guard duty and standing back to back with Kwan Yin. At the far end is an impressive red pagoda. When you have rested and seen this stage, you should continue up the steps to the higher level.

The first hall on the left as you reach this level houses the four Heavenly Kings (see page 72) who fill the hall with a riot of colour and symbolism so that you hardly notice the Taoist King of Heaven—the Jade Emperor—whom they are guarding. The shrine to the left of the four kings honours two Taoist warriors: Kwan Ti, the God of War in full battle array and mounted on a huge chestnut horse, and Chun Ti, a legendary character who could grow extra arms at will to help him defeat the enemy. The hall on the right is dedicated to Kwan Yin.

In the furthest temple on the highest level, you will find the gilded body of the founder of the temple and first abbot, enclosed in a glass case, looking extraordinarily small and frail in front of an immense standing gold Buddha who represents Amitabha (O Mi To Fat), Lord of the Western Paradise. The Reverend Yuet Ka graduated in 1897 from Shanghai and was immediately appointed professor of philosophy in Beijing. In the same year at the age of nineteen, he became a Buddhist monk and, in the course of a long life of teaching, wrote ninety-eight books on Buddhism. He died in 1965 at the age of eighty-seven and was buried in a coffin on the hillside behind the temple. When his body was exhumed eight months later, there was no sign of decomposition and so his awed followers decided to gild and enthrone the body for all to marvel at his sanctity that had defied the elements.

If you would like to return to Sha Tin Station by a different path, go back to the lower level and pass between the Lohans, keeping to the right-hand side. Beyond the statues there is a small stall selling drinks and sweet bean curd freshly made on the premises. Just beyond the stall is a flight of steps descending into the trees. If you follow the path heading downwards all the way and crossing a small stream, it will bring you out at the same old village houses that you passed earlier, and you will see the station above on the left.

It is possible to combine the Ten Thousand Buddha Temple with a visit to the Che Kung Temple and Tsang Tai Uk walled village, although the entire trip will include a couple of hours of walking. Leave the KCR at Tai Wai Station. If you don't wish to walk, you can take a taxi direct to Tsang Tai Uk.

Walkers should leave the station by the left-hand exit which is signposted to Che Kung Temple. Turn left and follow the footpath that runs parallel to the railway and around the bus terminus. Between the stalls selling fruit and souvenirs there is a path that leads down an underpass. Continue through the rather deserted pleasure complex, past some *dim sum* restaurants

and a small fairground and, bearing right, you will eventually come out at the end of a dead-end road. Already you will be able to see the large white concrete walls of the temple across Che Kung Miu Road to the right. Turn right and walk towards Che Kung Miu Road, crossing to the other side by way of the underpass (subway) and turning left as you come out. The temple is near the top of the underpass on the right.

The **Che Kung Temple** is modern and very well attended. The statue of the God himself is of gigantic proportions (see page 78 for his story). At a plague-ridden moment in Sha Tin's history, it was remarked that the villagers of Ho Po near Sai Kung never succumbed to epidemics and their good health was ascribed to the protection afforded by the village patron, Che Kung. Naturally though, the Ho Po villagers were unwilling to give away to Sha Tin so effective a protector. So a compromise was reached, and the name-plate of Che Kung's grandson was sent instead. Since then he has been as effective as his illustrious grandfather in keeping the people of Sha Tin free of epidemics. If you visit the temple at Chinese New Year, you can queue to turn the wheel which symbolizes both the cosmic movement in the turning of the year and the hope of each wheel spinner for a 'good turn' of fortune in the coming year.

To continue to Tsang Tai Uk, turn right out of the temple and follow Che Kung Miu Road, passing an attractive modern Buddhist temple. Cross Sha

Tsang Tai Uk

strongly lest the pirates should ever come back and seek revenge.

The three main gates, leading into the village, with their great iron-clad doors are still shut at night. Visitors are welcome to enter the first courtyard and look at the ancestral hall which is opposite the middle gate. The great wooden screen and the altar behind it appear somewhat dilapidated, but if you look carefully you are sure to be impressed by the beauty of the carving on both. The sides of the wooden screen contain lively carvings of the Eight Immortals (see pictures below and page 58–9). Notice the two wells at either end of the first courtyard to ensure drinking water in times of siege. The village,

Tin Tau Road by the underpass, then take the next underpass which will take you underneath Che Kung Miu Road, then back again. Make sure you come out on the far side of Lion Rock Tunnel Road on to a path with tennis courts on the left. The distinctive *wok-yee*-shaped corner towers (shaped like the handles of a wok) of **Tsang Tai Uk** will be in front of you. This fortified village is said to have taken twenty years to build, being ready for occupation in 1850. Tsang Koon Man, the founder (see page 16), is said to have made his money in a stone quarry. A different story relates how several jars filled with fish were left in his care by pirates with instructions that on no account should he touch them as they would soon return to recover them. When the pirates did not reappear, and the jars began to smell, he examined the contents and found in each a cache of silver coins. He built the village on the proceeds, fortifying it

Li Tie Guai with his crutch

Lu Dong Bin with his fly whisk

with its washing hanging outside and children playing safely, offers a very peaceful, friendly, and attractive appearance to visitors. The corner tower on the left as you leave the gates has recently been opened as an office where you can buy drinks. After you have seen the village, you can return to Tai Wai KCR Station, or continue further.

Half an hour's walk up Che Kung Miu Road turn right on to Yuen Chau Kok Road to reach an **old Chinese house** in Wong Uk village. This two-storey traditional brick building is over two hundred years old and was originally built as a trading station and place to stay for merchants and travellers. Recently renovated, it contains some fine murals and decorations, and is most attractive in its leafy green setting, with a small temple at its side. From here you can make your way to Sha Tin KCR Station by walking back along the Shing Mun River Channel and crossing the river at the Lek Yuen footbridge, built in the traditional Peking style.

PUBLIC TRANSPORT	
KMB	
80S	Kowloon Tong KCR station to Sui Wo Court via Lion Rock Tunnel Road
PUBLIC LIGHT BUS (Green)	
68K	Sha Tin KCR station to Julimount Gardens via Tai Wai KCR station, Che Kung Road, and Lion Rock Tunnel Road

CHAPTER 7

TAI PO MARKET

Tai Po has a very long history having been the centre of the pearl fishing industry for hundreds of years (see page 24). The name Tai Po means 'Big Strides'. The town is said to have come by its name because many hundreds of years ago on the outskirts of the town there grew a dense forest of gigantic trees among which lurked tigers and poisonous snakes. Villagers who needed to enter the forest for whatever purpose therefore urged each other to 'take big strides', to hurry to complete their mission. When the present road was being built through the district, the workmen uncovered the roots of huge old trees.

It is easier to take the KCR to Tai Po market than to go by car. When you alight at Tai Po Market station, descend the steps, then turn right and exit in front of Uptown Plaza. Turn right again and follow the covered walkway alongside the railway track until you reach Nam Wan Road. Turn right underneath the railway bridge and walk to the traffic lights, crossing the road at the pedestrian crossing and turning left into Heung Sze Wui Street. At the end of this road, cross Po Heung Street at the traffic lights, opposite the temporary market, then turn right. Next, take the first road on the left, Wai Yi Street. Cross at the intersection at the end of this road and continue up the hill along Shung Tak Street. A few metres along it on the right is Fu Shin Street, the main market street which is closed to traffic. If you continue a short way on up Shung Tak Street you will find the Railway Museum at the top of some wide steps on your left. The walk from the train to the market should not take much more than fifteen minutes.

The **Railway Museum** (No. 1 on the Central New Territories Country-side Series map) is situated in the old Tai Po Market station building designed

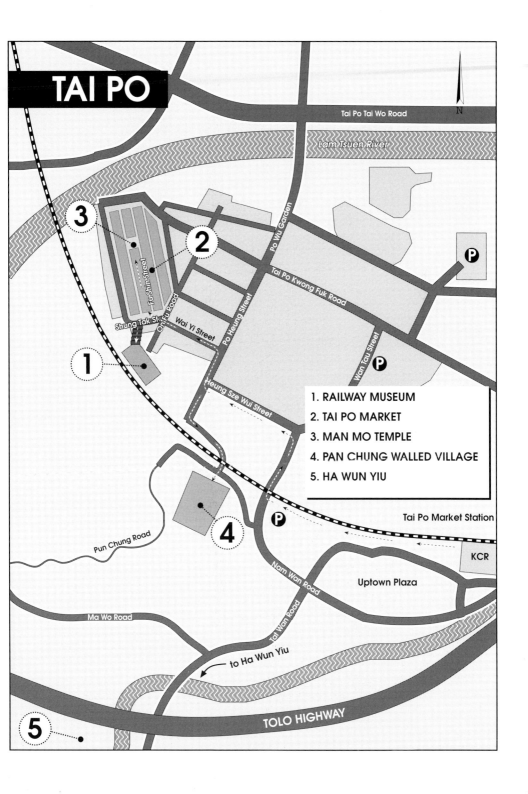

TAI PO

Tai Po Tai Wo Road

Lam Tsuen River

Po Wu Garden

Tai Po Kwong Fuk Road

Fu Shin Street

Shung Tak St.

On Fu Road

Wai Yi Street

Po Heung Street

Wan Tau Street

Heung Sze Wui Street

1. RAILWAY MUSEUM
2. TAI PO MARKET
3. MAN MO TEMPLE
4. PAN CHUNG WALLED VILLAGE
5. HA WUN YIU

Pun Chung Road

Tai Po Market Station

KCR

Uptown Plaza

Nam Wan Road

Tat Wan Road

Ma Wo Road

to Ha Wun Yiu

TOLO HIGHWAY

Entrance to Railway Museum

in the traditional old Chinese style. There are two old trains to look around as well as other exhibits and models.

The present **Tai Po Market** was established in the late nineteenth century by a group of villages, including Fanling, that wished to break the monopoly of the Tangs. The Tangs at that time allowed no one else to open shop in their market at the other end of the town. The new market was named the 'Market of Utmost Harmony' and it flourished from the very first day. You can find many cheap and useful purchases among the mounds of vegetables, medicines, and kitchenware, as well as more unusual items such as snake skins and live frogs.

The **Man Mo Temple** was built at the same time to mark the founding of the market. It lies three-quarters of the way down Fu Shin Street on the left-hand side, set back from the bustling market in its own courtyard flanked by palm trees—a haven of tranquillity. Inside it is hung with great coils of burning incense and its central open courtyard is filled with plants. Its attractive arches lead into passageways to the main altar. On the walls on either side of the altars are imposing examples of calligraphy. It is dedicated to Man Cheong and Kwan Ti (see page 76).

In order to see the walled village of **Pan Chung**, walk back the same way

Man Mo Temple

will find a fine ancestral hall with portraits of the ancestors and an altar kept bright with flowers and offerings.

Turn right as you leave the village and continue along the road until, very shortly, you will reach Nam Wan Road again. If you are ready to go back to the station, cross the road, turn left then first right, and return to the station along the same covered walkway that you came by.

If you want a longer walk, the village of **Ha Wun Yiu** is fifteen to twenty minutes' away. Turn right along Nam Wan Road until you come to a sizeable crossroads. Turn right again into Tat Wan Road and continue along it, making for the Tolo Highway viaduct in front of you. Shortly before you reach it you will come to some steps leading down to a nullah (water

you came until you reach the temporary market on Po Heung Street. Instead of turning down Heung Sze Wui Street, carry straight on, crossing the road and passing the Hong Kong Federation of Youth Groups Building. Then turn left along the road that follows the railway embankment. The path bends right under the railway and comes out just opposite the front gate of Pan Chung. As you go into the gatehouse, you will see the Earth God's shrine in the corner on the right. At the north end of the main lane is a small temple. From the gatehouse, turn down the second lane on the right. Here you

Entrance to Pan Chung

133

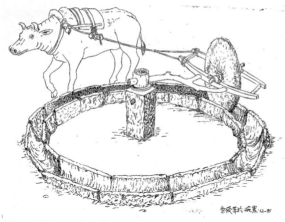

Water buffalo grinding China stone

china clay and china stone as well as water which could be mixed together to make porcelain paste. Excavation of the site in 1995 uncovered a small granite circular trough with a central granite post which was used for grinding china stone into powder. A water buffalo pulled a circular grinding blade around the trough. Remnants of bowls and moulds can still be seen all over the hillside.

course). Turn right along the path. After walking under the viaduct, you will reach a fork with a large telegraph pole in front of you. Take the small path on the right which sneaks away up the hillside, and climb the steps at the end. You will reach a concrete terrace with a **temple** and a former village school from where you can admire the excellent *fung shui* of their situation and outlook. The temple, built around 1790, is the only one in Hong Kong dedicated to Fan Sin, the God of Potters.

Continue on up the hill leaving the temple on your left. At the top of the steps, the path into the village of **Sheung Wun Yiu** bears left ahead of you. Instead you should go no further than the first large pink villa on the right and climb the steep steps alongside it. The hill on the left is the site of a **pottery** producing blue and white porcelain wares (see page 25). The hill contained rich deposits of

OPENING HOURS of the Railway Museum:

9 a.m. to 5 p.m. daily (including Sundays and Public Holidays)
Closed: Tuesdays, Christmas Day, Boxing Day, New Year's Day, and the first three days of Lunar New Year

PUBLIC TRANSPORT

PUBLIC LIGHT BUS (Green)

23K — Tai Po KCR station to San Uk Ka passing Ha Wun Yiu

134

ADDITIONAL PLACES OF INTEREST IN THE TAI PO AREA

Fong Ma Po is a village about two miles down the Lam Kam Road on the right-hand side if you are heading for Shek Kong. If you watch out as you drive you will see a large banyan tree set back from the road, hung with paper offerings. These papers are mainly hung around Chinese New Year and remain in the tree getting more and more tatty as the year goes on. If you stop and walk down the small road to the left of the tree, you will come to another bauhinia tree even more heavily festooned. Just beyond this tree is a very attractive **Tin Hau Temple** with a spirit wall in front of it and a red **Earth God Shrine** to the right of the temple. The temple has three halls and is obviously well used and cared for. If you visit Fong Ma Po during Chinese New Year you too can buy the proper paper packet of petitions and prayers, and throw them, weighted with a tangerine, as high as possible into the branches.

PUBLIC TRANSPORT	
Public Light Bus (Green)	
64K	Tai Po KCR station to Yuen Long West along Lam Kam Road passing Fong Ma Po
65K	Tai Po KCR station to Sheung Tsuen along Lam Kam Road passing Fong Ma Po

CHAPTER 8

TSUEN WAN

Tsuen Wan is very easy to get to by MTR and its sights are well planned and carefully preserved. It has a long and interesting history and in half a day you can see a historic Tin Hau temple, a fine example of an old Hakka clan home fortified against attackers, and a typical Chinese garden with the old village houses of Hoi Pa village preserved in its midst. For the visitor who would like a full day's sight-seeing, a minibus trip and a walk will allow you to compare a fine Taoist temple complex with a large and old Buddhist monastery.

The first place on the itinerary is the Tin Hau Temple. This is now situated in the corner of a large housing estate and walking through it gives one an opportunity to get a feeling of how a very large number of Hong Kong people live. The environment is well planned, clean, and pleasant. To walk to the temple leave Tsuen Wan station by Exit C. As you come out, take the escalator on the right of the square with a Park'n Shop supermarket at the top. After passing the front of the store and turning right, you will find an exit into the Luk Yeung Sun Chuen housing estate. Turn right on to a pedestrian walkway passing, after a few minutes, a fountain on your left then a children's playground on the right. Just before the end of the pedestrian walkway turn left along a narrow path. You will see the **Tin Hau Temple** up a flight of steps, hiding behind its spirit wall which is topped by two dragons vying for the pearl. As you round the spirit wall, you will find yourself in a courtyard with an outside altar and a large number of incense coils slowly burning. Watch out for falling ash as you pass underneath. This is the only temple I know where the coils of incence are burnt at a separate outside altar allowing the

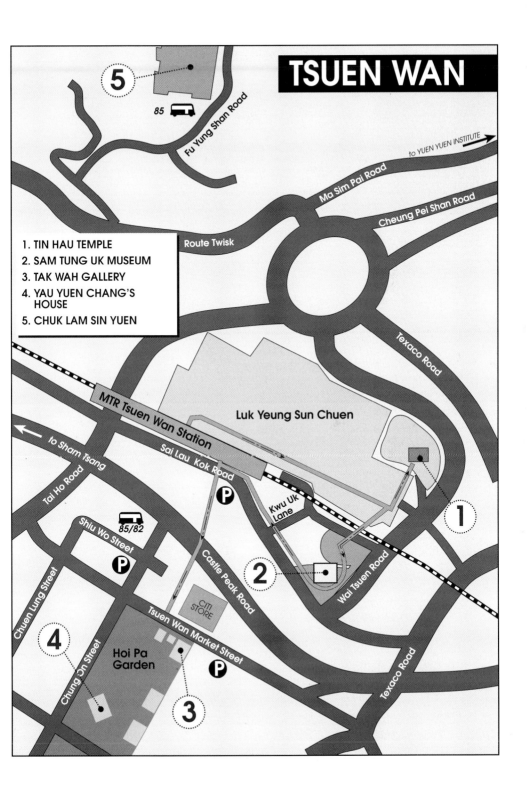

TSUEN WAN

1. TIN HAU TEMPLE
2. SAM TUNG UK MUSEUM
3. TAK WAH GALLERY
4. YAU YUEN CHANG'S HOUSE
5. CHUK LAM SIN YUEN

Fu Yung Shan Road

85

to YUEN YUEN INSTITUTE

Ma Sim Pai Road

Cheung Pei Shan Road

Route Twisk

Texaco Road

MTR Tsuen Wan Station

to Sham Tsang

Tai Ho Road

Sai Lau Kok Road

Luk Yeung Sun Chuen

Shiu Wo Street

85/82

Kwu Uk Lane

Chuen Lung Street

Castle Peak Road

Chung On Street

CITI STORE

Hoi Pa Garden

Tsuen Wan Market Street

Wai Tsuen Road

Texaco Road

5

1

2

4

3

P

Tin Hau Temple

After viewing the temple walk back along the same path, but this time keep straight on, crossing the footbridge at the end. This will lead you directly down to the back of the **Sam Tung Uk museum** (No. 7 on the central New Territories Countryside Series map). The path takes you round to the front of the museum through a garden with a pond and gatehouse on your left. The museum is set in a restored Hakka walled village. It was built in 1786 by a member of the Chan clan whose ancestors had emigrated from Fujian. The museum itself is attractively laid out to show various aspects of the Hakka lifestyle and often houses regional council exhibitions in the back rooms. It is well worth while taking the time to explore the rooms situated round the central clan hall.

Leave the Sam Tung Uk museum by the front pathway which goes down to the road. Walk back towards the station crossing Kwu Uk Lane. Take the stairs to the first pedestrian footbridge (walking a little way through the shopping centre), crossing over Sai Lau Kok Road. Stay on the footbridge, crossing Castle Peak Road, then entering the 'Town Square' shopping centre. The easiest way to reach the

interior to remain smoke free and clean.

The temple was rebuilt in 1846, but its bell dates from 1743. Over the entrance is a very detailed and intricate Shekwan pottery roof ridge and a finely carved gold-painted fascia board and *chai mun* (see page 80). The inside of the temple is richly ornamented with glass chandeliers and two fine multi-layered embroidered lanterns. The front of the altar is carved and gilded. Arranged on each side of the altar are eight red halberds with the emblems of the Eight Immortals, and two black halberds to the gods of literature and war respectively. In the hall to your right when facing the altar is a soul tablet honouring the seventeen Tsuen Wan villagers who died in the 1860s during the fighting between Tsuen Wan and the Shing Mun villagers (see page 16).

Hoi Pa Garden is to turn right into Citistore and descend by the shop's escalators to the ground floor. (You will know you have gone too far if you look down through the windows on the left of the covered footbridge and see the Hoi Pa Garden below.) The exit of Citistore is immediately opposite the entrance to the **Hoi Pa Garden**.

If you turn left on entering the gardens, you will pass a clan hall and, tucked into a corner beside it, an Earth God Shrine. Further on you will come to a row of old village houses. The middle one, the **Tak Wah Gallery**, is open to the public and houses a semi-permanent exhibition, entitled 'From Study Hall to Village School', showing Hong Kong's education systems through the ages. Look out for the corner in the first hall on the left showing a mock-up of Yau Yuen Chang (1865–1937) as a scholar studying for the Imperial Examination. He was born and educated in Hoi Pa village. His picture and a poem written by him as an exercise are both on show. When he failed the Imperial Examination he migrated to Jamaica and made his fortune there. On retiring, he came back to Tsuen Wan and built himself the house that you will find if you take the winding path that cuts diagonally across the garden to the south-west corner (facing away from the Tak Wah Gallery). This is a typical traditional house of the grander sort with some excellent plaster work friezes under the eaves. It is now used as an office and not open to the public.

Notice the layout of the whole garden which makes full use of the space to delight and surprise the visitor with its combination of water, rocks, trees, and shrubs to create a green oasis in the town centre. The goldfish in the ponds benefit from the many passersby who feed them and have grown impressively large. This brings you to the end of the tour. Make your way back to the MTR station by the same route.

Hoi Pa Garden

OPENING HOURS of the Sam Tung Uk Museum

9 a.m. to 4 p.m. daily (including Sundays and Public Holidays)
Closed: Tuesdays, Christmas Day, Boxing Day, New Year's Day, and the first three days of Lunar New Year.

ADDITIONAL PLACES OF INTEREST IN THE TSUEN WAN AREA

1. Yuen Yuen Institute

The minibus takes about ten minutes to reach the Yuen Yuen Institute (No. 6 on the central New Territories Countryside Series map) which is the last stop on its route. The valley you drive up must possess excellent *fung shui* judging by the number of temples found there. On the right as you go up the hill is **Western Monastery** which is in the process of building a nine-storey pagoda.

The Yuen Yuen Institute is the only temple complex I know dedicated to all three of the main religions practised in Hong Kong: Taoism, Buddhism, and Confucianism. It should be approached by its main gate which is a short way down the hill from the bus stop. You enter up steps through the archways, and on up past the very modern guardian lions to the main round temple. This temple is on two floors and is said to be modelled on the Temple of Heaven in Beijing—though it will not bear too close comparison. The lower hall accommodates a great number of images of the gods around the periphery of the building. In the upper hall the three founders of the three main religions practised in Hong Kong stand side by side with Sakyamuni, the founder of Buddhism, in the centre; Confucius on his right; and Laozi on his left. The ceiling of the upper hall is adorned with the *Baat*

Gwa (see page 22) with the *yin* and *yang* symbol at its centre

If you walk round the outside of the upper hall and out on to the higher level, you will find on your right a shrine to the Earth God and a tree to which worshippers have attached prayers by threads. To the right of this a very attractive pair of green dragons vye for a pearl shaped from growing bushes. To the left of the main temple you will find a statue of Kwan Yin above a rock on the right, and, on the left, a hall with an exhibition of beautiful rocks and stones, many of them strangely weathered. On the next terrace up is a hall dedicated to Kwan Ti, the God of War (see page 76), with a very intricate decorated ceiling. To the left of the hall is the statue of Confucius. Above and behind this terrace are a number of halls that serve as a resting place for the ashes of the deceased. If you turn left and walk a short way, you will find yourself back by the No. 81 minibus stop.

PUBLIC TRANSPORT		
PUBLIC LIGHT BUS (Green)		
81		Shiu Wo Street to Yuen Yuen Institute (circular)

2. Chuk Lam Sin Yuen

The walk to the Chuk Lam Sin Yuen (Bamboo Grove Monastery) takes less than half an hour and is not very

Chuk Lam Sin Yuen

road taking the left-hand fork down the hill. You will pass green and gold rooftops of monastery buildings on the left and, after crossing a bridge, will shortly reach a small square with a tree in the centre where you will see the entrance to the monastery on the right.

This monastery, founded in 1927, is one of the largest in Hong Kong. Inside the courtyard climb the steps on your left which take you to the entrance hall (see page 71). The main hall inside the courtyard and flanked by palm trees is very impressive. It houses the biggest Trikala (threesome) of Buddhas in the whole of Hong Kong. Sakyamuni sits in the centre facing south, with Yeuk Si Fat, the Healing Buddha and ruler of the Eastern Paradise, on his right and Amitabha, ruler of the Western Paradise, on his left. The eighteen Lohans line the sides of the hall, nine on each side. As you walk round to the back of the hall, you will find a large statue of Kwan Yin looking north. She is holding a willow branch in her hand with which to sprinkle healing water on those suffering from illness. On the rocks behind the main statue are many smaller statues of Kwan Yin in all her different forms.

strenuous. As you go down the road, on the right-hand side you will see a boat-shaped Buddhist temple rising from the bed of the stream. A path with red railings leads down off the road and passes it. Follow the path round and down until you come to a bridge over the stream with yellow railings. Cross the stream and ascend the path on the other side taking the steeper right-hand fork when the path divides. This path takes you up and then along beside a high fence topped with barbed wire on your left. Continue along this small path as it winds round the contours and then descends with rural housing on the right and a huge clearance (building) site on the left. The path eventually comes out into a square of parked cars with yellow painted houses on a granite terrace above the road on the right. Now follow the very narrow

As you come out of the main hall, immediately opposite is a rockery enclosed in a pool. This represents the happy land of the Western Paradise (see page 70). The Buddhas on the rocks are all smiling and raising their arms in joy. The house and vase at the bottom of the rock are surrounded by coins: a little slice of the happiness may go to those who can throw their coin into a window or into the vase. The big hall in the centre of the back row of buildings is dedicated to the founder of the monastery whose statue can be seen inside.

Leave the temple complex through the entrance hall and go down the steps. If you look to your right, you will see a square garden with a new statue to the increasingly popular Sei Min Fat or the Buddha who watches over the four directions. He is worshipped with flowers and scarves tied to the outer railings of his shrine. Gold leaf can be bought at the stalls which the keeper of the shrine sticks on to one of the four sides of the statue's plinth: this accounts for the brightness of the gold. The stall below the statue also makes very fine gilded paper lotus flowers to sell to the worshippers as offerings. The individual petals are dextrously folded and neatly positioned while one watches. It is now easy to make your way back to the minibus stand outside the monastery.

PUBLIC TRANSPORT

Public Light Bus (Green)

85	Shiu Wo Street to Chuk Lam Shim Yuen (circular)
81	Shiu Wo Street to Yuen Yuen Institute (circular)

CHAPTER 9

TUEN MUN

Tuen Mun is famous for its two monasteries, one Buddhist and the other Taoist. Both of the monasteries are clearly marked on the north-west New Territories Countryside Series map: Tsing Shan is No. 10 and Ching Chung Koon is No. 11.

One of the oldest and most interesting monasteries in Hong Kong is perhaps the **Tsing Shan Monastery** on the slopes of Castle Peak to the west of Tuen Mun. Tsing Shan means Green Mountain because it is said that when a drought affects the territory and all the other hilltops are bare and brown, that particular hill always remains green.

The monastery owes its fame to a legendary monk called Pui To who, in about AD 428, told the family he was ministering to that he had to go to Guangdong and would never see them

again. Whereupon, and not for the first time, he threw his wooden drinking cup upon the sea and sailed away in it to the Tsing Shan Monastery where he became the abbot. His name Pui To is derived from his legendary exploit and means 'cup across' or 'cup ferry'. There are many stories of the miracles he carried out and the sicknesses he cured. Once, after staying for six months with a poor scholar and sharing his very meagre food, Pui To instructed the man to provide thirty-six rice baskets. The

Entrance to Tsing Shan Monastery

143

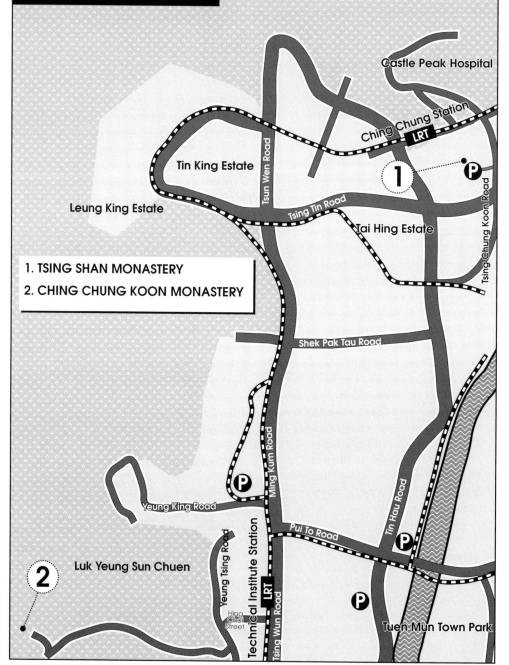

TUEN MUN

Castle Peak Hospital

Ching Chung Station
LRT

Tin King Estate

Tsun Wen Road

Leung King Estate

Tsing Tin Road

Tai Hing Estate

Tsing Chung Koon Road

(1)

P

1. TSING SHAN MONASTERY
2. CHING CHUNG KOON MONASTERY

Shek Pak Tau Road

Ming Kum Road

Tin Hau Road

P

Yeung King Road

P

Yeung Tsing Road

Technical Institute Station

Pui To Road

P

Luk Yeung Sun Chuen

(2)

LRT

Tsing Wun Road

Hing Che Street

P

Tuen Mun Town Park

poor man spent the last of his money and was able to secure only ten whereupon the remaining twenty-six materialized around the house. Pui To told the man to wrap each basket separately and then he left. When the baskets were later unwrapped, they were found to be overflowing with coins.

The monastery finally fell into disuse in the early nineteenth century and was used for a time as a Taoist temple. It was re-established in 1918 but has not prospered. The last monk died not long ago and it now seems to be cared for by some nuns. It is a haven of peace and well worth a visit. Behind the temple, is the Pui To Pavilion with a statue of Pui To high up at the very back under the rocks. A military officer is said to have paid a local stone mason to carve the statue in AD 945, although it is hard to believe that it is really so old, as it has recently been repainted. A new statue of Sei Min Fat, the Buddha facing four ways, has been placed in the centre of the pavilion. At the top of some more steps to the right you will find a temple to Kwan Yin. To the left of this temple at the far end of a narrow cave is a statue of Pao Kung or Justice Pao (AD 999–1062) who achieved fame as a shrewd and impartial magistrate in the Song dynasty. To his right is Yueh Lao, the divine matchmaker, well supplied with red thread. This god uses the thread to bind the ankles even before birth of those babies that he feels are suited to marry each other.

Yueh Lao with his reels of red thread

There are wonderful views over Tuen Mun and the sea. An arbour called Hoi Yuet Ting or 'Sea Moon Arbour' was built on the upper level for the purpose of looking at the moonlight over the sea, although the view is now obscured by trees. The Buddhist monks who revere all forms of life used to buy live fish in the market and release them into the sea. Some fish died anyway, and, for them, the monks had a special Fish Tomb built.

If you follow the path to the top of the hill, at the summit you will find a large stone carved with the characters, *Ko Shan Tai Yat*, meaning 'most excellent high peak'. It is supposed to have been written by a famous scholar of the Tang Dynasty, Hon Yue (AD 768–824).

PUBLIC TRANSPORT	
LRT	
506	Ferry pier to Yau Oi (alight at Technical Institute)
610	Ferry pier to Yuen Long terminus
615	Ferry pier to Yuen Long terminus

The **Ching Chung Koon Monastery** is easy to get to both by car and by public transport. If you take the ferry to Tuen Mun, it is simple to pick up the LRT, and to get off at the Ching Chung Koon Monastery stop.

Ching Chung Koon Monastery

If you come by car from Tsuen Wan, take the third exit off the Tuen Mun Highway to Tuen Mun West, turning into Tsing Tin Road. If approaching from Yuen Long, Tsing Tin Road is the first turning off the Highway to Tuen Mun. Then take the first turning to the left down Tsun Wen Road. Take the first left again on to Tsing Choon Koon Road which will take you around a playing field, then underneath the highway you were on earlier. The monastery is the first turning on the left, almost opposite Tuen Mun Hospital. The monastery has a car park where, for a small fee, you can leave your car.

This monastery is Taoist and fairly modern although it is built in a very traditional style, with its golden curving roof. Before going into the main temple, do not forget to look up at the intricate and highly decorated roof structure. It is built according to age-old rules concerning weight dispersal and is very similar in construction to ancient temple roofs found all over China. The main temple hall is dedicated to Lu Dong Bin, the second of the Eight Immortals (see page 58), and contains many treasures including lanterns from Beijing's Imperial Palace. The halberds in the front of the temple bear the symbols of the Eight Immortals. To the right of the temple entrance doors is a useful plaque giving detailed information about the layout of the temple.

The monastery is also rightly famed for the beauty of its amazing bonsai

Shekwan pottery figures

which they grow. Below the café is a small, but very classical and well-laid out, typical Chinese garden (see page 64)

Within the grounds of the monastery are two homes for the aged, and two Chinese medicine clinics which dispense free medicine to the needy. There is also a restaurant serving typical Chinese vegetarian dishes and a café for meat-free snacks and drinks. The entire complex is run by the Ching Chung Koon Taoist Association which was founded in 1949 and has sister organizations in the United States, Japan, Taiwan, Australia, and Canada. The association also runs two kindergartens, one primary school, and one secondary school.

The monastery also acts as a Temple of Remembrance with three halls where the Taoist priests conduct ceremonies for the dead. You will see that the walls are lined with plaques, often bearing photographs of the departed, so that family members can come to pay their respects whenever they want.

tree collection and the skill of its gardeners. The different species of tree, ways of growing them, and variety of pots is breathtaking. Many of the miniature bonsai landscapes include Shekwan pottery figures. Some of the bonsai trees on display are very much older than any of the buildings among

PUBLIC TRANSPORT

LRT	
505	Sam Shing terminus to Siu Hong (alight at Ching Chung)
610	Ferry pier to Yuen Long terminus (alight at Tuen Mun Hospital and walk around the hospital)
615	Ferry pier to Yuen Long terminus (alight at Ching Chung)

CHAPTER 10

SAI KUNG

For a relaxing day away from the smog and high rises, head for Sai Kung town and Sheung Yiu Folk Museum, just inside the **Sai Kung Country Park**.

The entrance to the country park at **Pak Tam Chung** is about five kilometres beyond Sai Kung, and it makes sense to start from here and then drive back to Sai Kung later where you will find a wide variety of eating places. Leave the car in one of the large car parks provided on the left-hand side of the road, before the country park barrier. The Country Park Visitor Centre near the entrance to the park has an excellent display of materials on the history, geology, flora, and fauna of the area. You can also purchase the **Pak Tam Chung Nature Trail** pamphlet there which will add considerable interest to the walk to the museum.

Walk into the country park along the road beyond the barrier, keeping to the right-hand side. After about five minutes, just before you reach the first small noodle and drinks stall, you will see a path down to the right leading over a bridge. The **Sheung Yiu Folk Museum** is about a kilometre down this path which also has twenty marked points on the nature trail along it. You can see, for example, the *Heong* or Incense Tree that gave its name to Hong Kong (see page 23), as well as a number of interesting and useful plants, such as the Sandpaper Vine used for polishing chopsticks. Number 15 is an old lime kiln. Lime making, using shells or coral, mixed with charcoal and layered with dried grass, was an important local industry, employing many workers. The lime was used for, among other things, plastering the walls and ceilings of local houses.

The village hamlet itself, with its narrow fortified entrance guarded by a watchtower, has been well restored

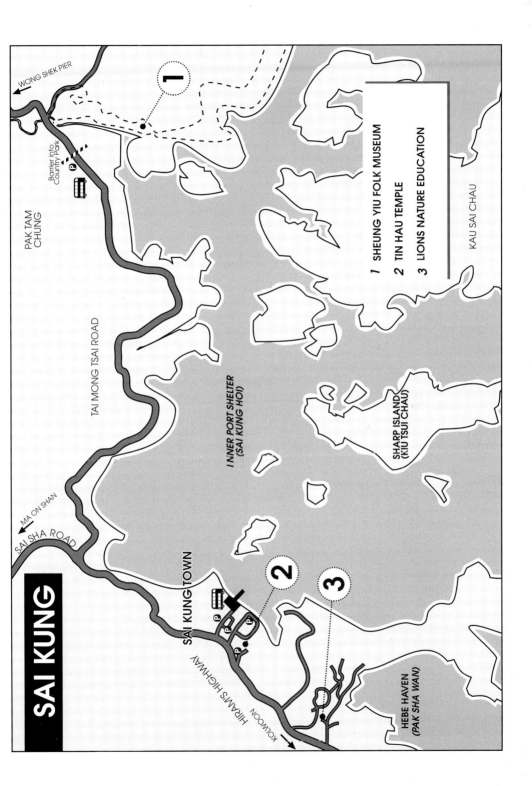

SAI KUNG

WONG SHEK PIER

Barrier into Country Park

PAK TAM CHUNG

TAI MONG TSAI ROAD

MA ON SHAN

SAI SHA ROAD

SAI KUNG TOWN

HIRAM'S HIGHWAY

KOWLOON

INNER PORT SHELTER (SAI KUNG HOI)

SHARP ISLAND (KIU TSUI CHAU)

HEBE HAVEN (PAK SHA WAN)

KAU SAI CHAU

1 SHEUNG YIU FOLK MUSEUM

2 TIN HAU TEMPLE

3 LIONS NATURE EDUCATION

Sheung Yiu village

attractive and relatively unspoilt old market town with typical Chinese medicine, dried sea food, and incense shops. You can dine outside on the busy sea front on freshly cooked sea food you have chosen yourself from the tanks, and watch the boats.

You should allow enough time to see the **Tin Hau Temple**. There has been a temple on this site for around seven hundred years, acting as the centre of local activities

and furnished to give a vivid impression of local life in the earlier part of this century. The last of the Wong family left in 1965 and they are now settled in Britain.

You can either return by the way you came, or, if you prefer a longer and more strenuous walk, continue along the path until you come to some steps on the left leading up the hill. This is the **Sheung Yiu Family Walk**. Climb to the top of the steps where you will see a signpost in Chinese characters. Take the track to the left, rather than continuing up the steps on the right. Follow the 'Family Trail' signs (showing three people). The walk is about two kilometres long and will lead you back to the road. Turn left, and after about half a kilometre you'll be back at the car park.

It is worth allowing time to explore the town of **Sai Kung**. This is an

Tin Hau Temple

150

and organizations. Before entering notice the frieze of a pair of mandarin ducks swimming happily among the lotus plants under the roof eaves—a symbol of marital happiness. The bats on either side of the main doors also symbolize happiness. One hall is dedicated to Tin Hau and the other to Kwan Ti, God of War and Righteousness (see page 76). The temple is obviously well used and cared for. During the last restoration (1994) about half the funds collected to pay the expenses came from addresses in Britain.

The Lion's Nature Education Centre is off Hiram's Highway, south of Sai Kung. In the far corner of the Centre is a potted garden showing a wide variety of medicinal plants all labelled with their names and uses.

OPENING HOURS of Lion's Nature Education Centre:

9.30 a.m. to 5 p.m. daily
Closed: Tuesdays

OPENING HOURS of Sheung Yiu Folk Museum:

9 a.m. to 4 p.m. daily
Closed: Tuesdays, Christmas Day, Boxing Day, New Year's Day, first three days of Chinese New Year

PUBLIC TRANSPORT
At Choi Hung MTR station exit to Clearwater Bay Road North

KMB	
92	Choi Hung to Sai Kung Town
94	Sai Kung to Wong Shek pier
96R	Choi Hung to Wong Shek pier via Pak Tam Chung (Sundays and public holidays only)

Public Light Bus (Green)	
1 & 1A	Choi Hung Public Transport Terminus to Sai Kung Town
9	Sai Kung to Maclehose Holiday Village stopping at Pak Tam Chung

ADDITIONAL PLACES OF INTEREST IN THE SAI KUNG AREA

1. Tin Hau Temple, Joss House Bay
This, the oldest temple site in Hong Kong, is in a very dramatic and unspoilt position overlooking the sea. The first temple was built by the Lam brothers in 1012 to give thanks to Tin Hau for their survival in a shipwreck off the

151

Tin Hau Temple

The path to the temple is to be found at the very end of Clearwater Bay Road where a barrier marks the entrance to the Clearwater Bay Golf Club. On the right a path descends through the trees. If you arrive by bus, it will take you about twenty-five minutes to walk from the terminus along the road to the temple.

coast. They are said to have survived by clinging to a statue of Tin Hau who carried them safely ashore. This temple was built in 1266 by the brothers' descendants. It has been rebuilt and enlarged many times but, according to the inscription over the entrance, the present building dates from 1878. The temple is a favourite with the boat people, and, on the birthday of Tin Hau in May, hundreds of boats come here to pay their respects, all decked out in multi-coloured flags.

Just behind the temple on the path down from Clearwater Bay Road is a historic rock carving dating from 1274 giving details of a visit paid by an official of the Song Dynasty only a very short time before its final defeat by the Mongol army. The text, consists of 108 characters in very fine calligraphy and is deeply incised on the rock. A translation in English is provided nearby.

PUBLIC TRANSPORT	
KMB	
91	Choi Hung to Clearwater Bay

2. Tap Mun Chau (Grass Island)

For an adventurous day out, you cannot choose a more enjoyable destination than Tap Mun Chau. The road to Wong Shek Pier passes through Sai Kung Country Park. Private cars need a permit to drive through the country park, so it is easier to take the bus. From the upper deck, you will get an impression of the wonderful walks possible on either side of the road. At the pier, you can wait for the ferry or, if the timing is wrong, take a *kai do* (small boat) and speed through the water, clutching your hat and glasses, to the island.

Standing above the little fishing village is a very old and beautiful **Tin Hau Temple**. When you leave the ferry pier, take the path to the left passing the New Hon Kee Restaurant which is highly recommended for the freshness of its delicious sea food. At the next crossroads you will see the temple above you. It is said to have been built between 1662 and 1723, and has been sympathetically restored. Over the inner door hangs a great

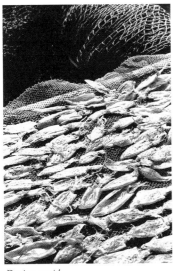

Drying squid

carved *chai mun* and on either side of the smoke well are two wonderful friezes of Shekwan pottery, dated 1888. You should also examine the carved front of the central altar with its vivid scenes from the last century. To the left of the Tin Hau Temple is a shrine to Kwan Ti, with a papier-mâché horse provided for him to ride. On the right

of the temple is the Water and Moon Palace dedicated to Kwan Yin (see page 71). On her altar is an old bronze sounding block dated 1788.

If you follow the path on up above the temple you will come out at a viewing pavilion with wonderful views of sea and hills. From there you can do a circuit of the island, or retrace your steps and walk along the path to the right of the ferry pier which will take you to the New Fisherman Village. You will see everywhere signs of the importance of the sea in the lives of the inhabitants.

PUBLIC TRANSPORT

At Choi Hung MTR station exit to Clearwater Bay Road North

KMB

| 94 | Sai Kung to Wong Shek pier |
| 96R | Choi Hung to Wong Shek pier via Pak Tam Chung (Sundays and public holidays only) |

Public Light Bus (Green)

| 7 | Pak Tam Chung to Hoi Ha (alight at the junction of Wong Shek pier and walk) (Sundays and Public Holidays only) |

CHAPTER 11

LANTAU

Lantau literally means
'broken head' but is
usually referred to in
Cantonese as *Dai Yue Shan*—'Big
Island Mountain'. At 142 square
kilometres it is twice the size of Hong
Kong. You will need a full day spare to
make a visit worthwhile, if possible
avoiding a Sunday when the influx of
visitors puts more strain on the public
transport system. If you want to
imagine how Hong Kong was before
the Second World War, Lantau will give
you a good idea. The still unspoilt
beauty of its mountains and the charm
of its old fishing villages make it a
destination not to be missed.

If you arrive by ferry at Silvermine
Bay (Mui Wo) it pays not to dawdle
getting off the boat. The bus terminus
is opposite the ferry pier, and the buses
wait for the boat and leave when they
are full. The names of the different
destinations are clearly visible above
. the various bus shelters. The buses take

about forty-five minutes to
reach the Po Lin Monastery at
Ngong Pin or Tai O, and a
good half hour to get to Tung
Chung.

The Po Lin Monastery

This Buddhist Monastery boasts the
largest Buddha in East Asia. After about
half an hour on the bus, you will pass
the Shek Pik Reservoir on your right. If
you look up above it, along the skyline
you will see the vast statue sitting
serenely on its plinth surveying the
view towards China. Po Lin means
'precious lotus', the lotus being the
symbol for purity. The monastery was
founded around 1920 by three reclusive
monks as a place of retreat. Other
monks joined them and the monastery
was formally inaugurated in 1928.

Once you arrive there are two
places to visit: the big Buddha, and the
monastery itself. The immense Buddha

The Buddha from Po Lin Monastery

Sakyamuni sits on his lotus throne at the top of a great flight of stairs (268 steps). His left hand resting in his lap symbolizes charity or the bestowing of gifts, while the right hand is raised in blessing. Made of bronze, the Buddha alone stands twenty-six metres tall and weighs 250 tonnes. It was cast in 202 numbered pieces in a factory in Nanjing, China.

At the top, on both sides of the stairway, stand six magnificent Boddhisattva statues (see page 68–9) each making different offerings to Buddha. The six offerings are incense, flowers, light, scented ointment, fruit, and musical instruments; they represent the six practices that lead to enlightenment.

Inside the Buddha itself are three levels. The lowest level, the Hall of Virtue, is open free to all visitors. In order to visit the more interesting upper halls, you need to buy a ticket which will also entitle you to a free Buddhist vegetarian meal. In the centre, linking the halls, a stairway winds up round a beautiful old statue of the Earth God made of yellow nanmu wood (*c.* AD 1500). Above the statue is a huge computer-controlled bell.

The second level shows an oil painting which is said to be the largest in the world made up of eighty-two jointed pieces showing the life of Buddha. Some fine pieces of Chinese art and calligraphy are on display round this hall. The third level contains the inscribed names of all those who contributed to the project and an altar on which a golden lotus is displayed holding in its centre a holy Buddhist relic from Sri Lanka. The view from the platform at the top of the stairway is breathtaking on a clear day and makes the climb all the more worthwhile.

The monastery is laid out in a very traditional manner and was built in 1970. First you pass through a sub-hall where you will be greeted by Maitreya, the laughing Buddha (see pages 70–1) surrounded by guardians. Behind the Laughing Buddha is a statue of Wei To (see page 72). Beyond this room stands the main hall, splendid with its gold paint and green tiles, standing high on its platform above a flight of stairs. The hall's three main statues are three metres high, carved from wood and encased in gold leaf. Sakyamuni sits in

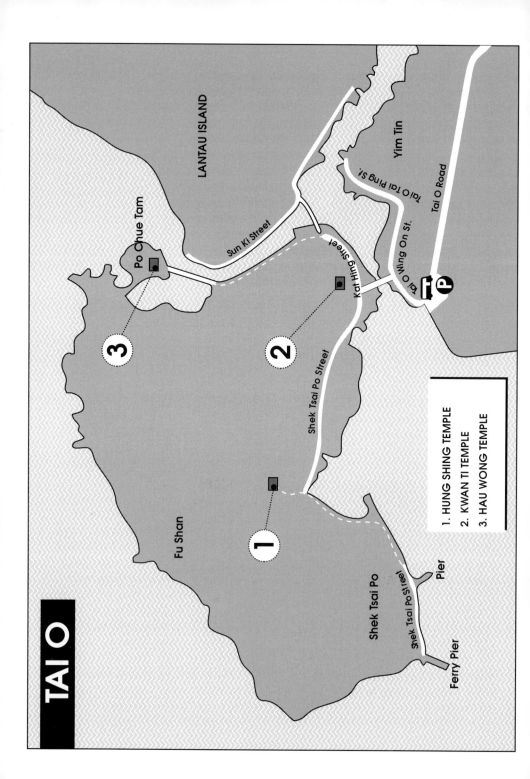

TAI O

LANTAU ISLAND

Yim Tin

Tai O Road

Tai O Tai Ping St.

Tai O Wing On St.

Sun Ki Street

Po Chue Tam

3

Kat Hing Street

2

Shek Tsai Po Street

Fu Shan

1

Shek Tsai Po

Shek Tsai Po Street

Pier

Ferry Pier

P

1. HUNG SHING TEMPLE
2. KWAN TI TEMPLE
3. HAU WONG TEMPLE

the centre, flanked by the Healing Buddha on his right and the Lord of Western Paradise on his left (see page 73). Kwan Yin, Goddess of Mercy, stands at the back. Behind the main hall is the original chamber where the monks still pray at 5 a.m. and 3 p.m. In this hall, you will see the founding Buddha, Sakyamuni, with his father and son standing behind him. The statue of Sakyamuni is made of white neophrite and was brought here from Thailand in 1925.

Tai O

Tai O village is one of the best preserved places in the whole of Hong Kong, and has a unique atmosphere of the sea, fishing, and quiet friendliness. It is mainly inhabited by Tanka families (see page 3), and the houses are built on stilts on either side of the creek. Every house has its boat tied up underneath and you can often see rattan baskets of fish or prawns hanging out to dry in the sun. You will notice a large number of shops specializing in all sorts of dried sea foods. Tai O is a favourite destination for Hong Kong people wanting to stock up on these items. It used to be the centre of a flourishing salt industry and you can see the disused salt pans looking like huge shallow fishponds on both sides of the town (see page 24). Besides this, Tai O has no less than four temples, two of which are included in this tour.

From Po Lin Monastery you will have to take a taxi down the mountainside to Tai O. If you are coming from the ferry pier at Mui O, catch the bus to Tai O. When you reach the village, follow the crowds down towards the sea and fishing boats. You will see that most people turn left down a narrow street lined with stalls that runs parallel to the river. Follow this street for a few minutes until it winds to the left down to the river itself. Then make your way over the new hump-backed drawbridge to the opposite bank of the river. Keep walking straight on up the main road, Tai O Market Street, with shop houses on either side until you come to a T-

Sea food drying in Tai O

Hau Wong Temple, Tai O

junction, where you meet Kat Hing Street. Both ways are very enjoyable to explore. The left-hand path will lead you to the Tsuen Wan ferry pier and a newly renovated but very old **Hung Shing Temple** standing back on the right of the path about half a mile from the junction. But if you want to see two more temples, including perhaps the most beautifully situated in Hong Kong, you should turn right.

Almost immediately, on your left, you will find a temple with an old and very fine Shekwan pottery roof ridge. This temple has stood on this site since the reign of Hong Zhi (1488–1505) in the Ming Dynasty, though of course it has been renovated many times. It is dedicated to **Kwan Ti** (see page 76), the God of War and of Righteousness. As you enter you will see two horses, one on each side of the temple. The one on the right belongs to Kwan Ti himself and the one on the left to the

emperor, Liu Pei, whom he served. The great bronze bell that hangs on the right of the temple was cast in 1739.

Leaving the temple, turn left and continue along Kat Hing Street. As you walk down the street, notice the many stone shrines to the Earth God. You will also see on your left an old style house with wooden folding doors. Continue on keeping right and cross over a causeway. From here you will see, on the other side, nestling under its *fung shui* woods, perhaps the most picturesque temple in the whole of Hong Kong. It is dedicated to **Hau Wong** (see page 77). As you enter you will see the Earth God shrine on the left of the main hall, and, on the right, fossils of sharks' bones and a whale's head. Notice the fine Shekwan pottery pictures in the centre of the temple on each side of the smoke well.

It is rewarding to explore Tai O in almost any direction. On the way back,

LANTAU

about half way along Kat Hing Street, turn left by the road sign on house number 36 and walk down Sun Ki Street to the bridge. From here you will have a very good view of the houses on stilts built on both banks of the creek. Despite their lack of modern comforts, very few locals have applied to live in the government-built blocks of flats on the edge of Tai O. Most of these new flats remain vacant, and the government is now considering selling them to private enterprise.

Tung Chung

Tung Chung has always been a small, sleepy agricultural settlement of great charm. Its one moment of fame in the history of Hong Kong was in the thirteenth century when it gave refuge to the Song court and the two boy emperors (see page 4). According to local legend, a number of locals are descendants of court members. But sadly its rural peace is set to change with the new airport right on its doorstep, as well as the new town of Tung Chung. However its two main attractions should be preserved. Ask the bus driver to set you down at **Tung Chung Fort** which is one stop and about half a mile from the bus terminus. Cross the road, and almost opposite you will see a small path with a signpost to the fort which is a couple of minutes walk from the road.

The fort was completed in 1832 and

Tung Chung Fort

measures 70 metres by 80 metres. It is enclosed on three sides by walls built of granite blocks which are wide enough for five people to walk abreast along the top. The fourth side is secured by the mountain rising at the back. The walls are pierced by arched gateways on all three sides and topped by small guardhouses for the lookouts. Along the front of the fort are six old muzzle-loading canons, all dating from the last century. This fort, at the strategically important mouth of the Pearl River, is witness to the turbulent past of the area and the need to keep pirates and other marauders in check. For many years the fort housed Tung Chung primary school and must have made a delightfully quiet and green site for a school. An information centre displaying the history of the fort is open to the public.

Walk back to the main road and cross over to the track across the fields. Follow this track and, where it joins a slightly wider path, turn left and continue down it passing an Earth God shrine on your right. Ten to fifteen minutes walk will bring you out at the **Hau Wong Temple**. This small quiet temple looks out to sea over a grassy foreshore and has an air of tranquillity. It has recently been renovated and is decorated in bright colours that belie its age. The bell was cast in 1765, so the temple must have been built around that time.

Walk back along the same path you came by, but this time do not turn right. Instead keep straight on, walking round a construction site. Eventually, the path will lead you through the village of Tung Chung until you arrive at the ferry pier and bus terminal. You will pass a number of simple eating places where you can get drinks or rice and noodle dishes while waiting for your bus back to Mui Wo.

A few minutes walk up the road from the bus terminal is, on the left, the site of the Tung Chung Battery which is also a listed monument. When I visited it, the site was very overgrown and there was little to see except the surrounding walls. There is little doubt that it is the site of one of the two batteries built in 1817 and listed in the Guangdong Annals.

CHAPTER 12

CHEUNG CHAU

If you are short of time and want to get a taste of Chinese culture away from the noise and bustle of the high rises, with a trouble free and relaxing journey, you cannot do better than take a trip to Cheung Chau—particularly if you avoid the weekends and public holidays.

On leaving the ferry pier, immediately to your right there is an excellent metal map of the island which makes it easy to get your bearings. The walk to the Temple of Jade Vacuity takes less than ten minutes, and this, being the richest and best-known temple in Cheung Chau, is a good place to begin the tour. Turning left out the ferry pier exit, proceed along the waterfront (Praya Street) with the harbour on your left. You will see a large number of fishing boats at anchor and all sorts of activities connected with the sea, which has for centuries provided a living for the majority of the islanders.

A short distance after the waterfront bends to the left, you will find, on the right-hand side, a concrete football pitch and, to its right, a large square marked out for basketball. On the far side of this, up a flight of steps, you will see the **Temple of Jade Vacuity**, built in 1783. Before you go into the temple, take a look at the roof

Temple of Jade Vacuity

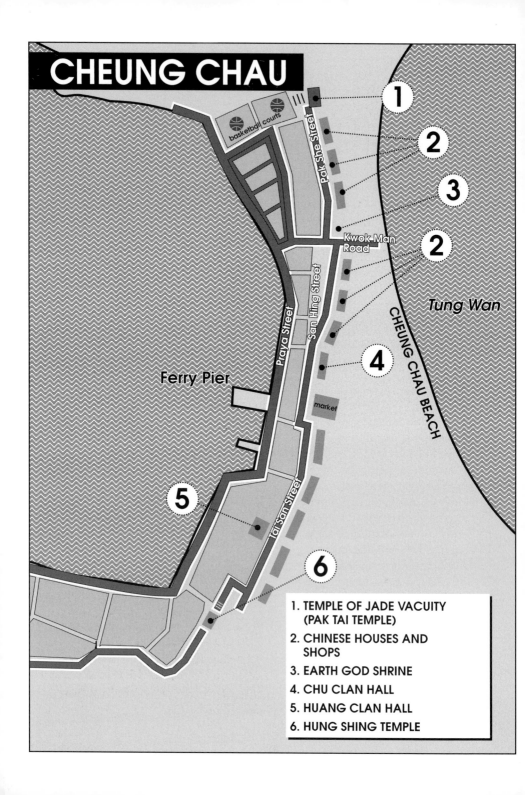

CHEUNG CHAU

1
2
3
2

basketball courts

Pak She Street

Kwok Man Road

Tung Wan

San Hing Street

Praya Street

Ferry Pier

CHEUNG CHAU BEACH

4

market

5

Tai San Street

6

1. TEMPLE OF JADE VACUITY
   (PAK TAI TEMPLE)

2. CHINESE HOUSES AND
   SHOPS

3. EARTH GOD SHRINE

4. CHU CLAN HALL

5. HUANG CLAN HALL

6. HUNG SHING TEMPLE

Dragon pillars

Northern Heavens (see page 76). He sits in the central position at the back of the temple with the snake and tortoise under his bare feet. Standing in front of the altar are the two guardian generals: 'Thousand *Li* Eyes' (on the right) has amazing long-distance eyesight, while 'Favourable Wind Ear' has exceptionally sharp hearing. To the left of the main altar in a glass case against the wall is a precious, iron sword discovered by local fishermen and dedicated to Pak Tai. It is believed to have been forged in the Song Dynasty and is five feet long with a three-inch blade. Leaning against the wall are the eight metal halberds carried in processions. Each one bears the emblem of one of the Immortals (see page 58). On either side of the temple is an opening, one round and the other square. Through these openings, you can see life-sized plaster mouldings, to the left of the White Tiger and to the right the Jade Dragon (see page 7).

This temple comes into its own during the Bun Festival which is usually held in early May. Pak Tai himself selects the date which is revealed through divination. The festival is held to commemorate Pak Tai's intervention to quell an outbreak of plague in 1777. (There is a good description in *Chinese Festivals* by Joan Law and Barbara Ward, page 48). The Bun Festival, which lasts a week, with a climax of Chinese opera and colourful processions, is well worth taking time to visit.

ridge and the brightly coloured plaster mouldings along the front of the newly restored temple. On each side of the doorway there are very fine gilded carved wood decorations and, within the entrance itself, is an intricately carved and gilded *chai mun* (see page 80), elegantly roofed, with two-tiers filled with legendary people and a phoenix at either end.

After you enter the temple, take a good look at the two finely carved stone pillars. You will see the pearl in the mouth of the very expressive guardian dragons that writhe up the full length of the pillars. The temple itself is dedicated to Pak Tai, the Supreme Emperor of the Dark

When you have descended the steps of the temple, turn immediately to your left and leave the concrete square via the vehicle barrier. A little to your right you will find yourself in **Pak She Street**. Continue down this street, noting the fine Chinese house almost immediately on the left-hand side with its barred wooden doorway and attendant stone lions. At numbers 25 and 32 you will find two different forms of Chinese medicine. Number 25 is a bone doctor, specializing in bone manipulation and the setting of broken limbs. Number 32 is a general physician, who cures diseases with special regimes of herbs, diets, exercises, and acupuncture. At the junction of Pak She Street and Kwok Man Road, you will see a red-painted altar to the **Earth God** whose large triangular rock sits in the centre behind the joss stick container. Pak She Street ends here and San Hing Street begins a little to the left, running parallel to the sea front.

San Hing Street is another narrow road where you can also find signs of a traditional Chinese lifestyle. On the right-hand side at number 56 is a herbalist shop, displaying many kinds of dried leaves and twigs. If you feel in need of a cooling herbal draught, you can buy one at this shop. The taste is a little bitter and distinctly medicinal. The **Chu clan's ancestral hall** is set back between numbers 36 and 38. Further down, on the left at number 68 (among others) there is an incense shop selling all the things necessary for worshipping the Gods. The small brown blocks in front of the shop are blocks of sweet smelling sandalwood. Number 80 on the same side of the road caters for the needs of the fishing fraternity. Among the myriad other goods, you will find the typical bamboo hats, equally effective against sun or rain. The round brimmed ones belong to the Tanka people whose ancestors, one of the earliest groups to make their home in Hong Kong, probably came from modern Vietnam. The conical hats are worn by the Hoklo people who came from the coastal province of Fujian to the north of Hong Kong (see page 1). Continue past the market on your left, turning left behind it, then right on to **Hing Lung Main Street**, and continue walking in the same direction. Hing Lung Main Street becomes **Tai San Street** at the intersection. Opposite number 30 you will see the **Huang clan's ancestral hall**. When you've nearly reached the end of the street, take the last turning on the right, then turn left and climb a few steps. Turn right at the top to reach the Hung Shing Temple.

The **Hung Shing Temple** was built in 1813 to honour the sea deity, Hung Shing Kung (see page 78). Notice the well-adorned Shekwan roof ridge with dragon fish, and two dragons vying for the sacred pearl on the upper level, and a busy scene of Gods and heroes in pavilions underneath. The wealth and standing of this temple are shown by the granite columns and supports with their guardian lions and the imposing granite door surrounds. Notice the golden bats symbolizing happiness on either side of the door above the gold painted couplets. The raised, red painted board across the doorway is there to keep out evil spirits. This temple may not be as grand as the Temple of Jade Vacuity but it is more of a community temple and you are likely to see worshippers coming and going about their business with the gods.

From this temple, if you walk in the direction in which it looks out you will very soon come to the sea, and by turning right along the sea front you will soon arrive back at the ferry pier. If you would like a longer, more energetic walk, take the Sai Wan Road to Sai Wan at its very end, turning right along the harbour. If you prefer to go by boat catch a *kai do* from the small ferry pier on the waterfront. There are two attractions to see, both well signposted from Sai Wan: an old **Tin Hau Temple** with a fine Shekwan pottery roof ridge and a **Tin Hau Pavilion** looking out over the sea. From here you can follow the signs to a rocky area with some caves with rather narrow entrances where the pirate, Cheung Po Tsai (see page 14) is said to have hidden his treasure. You can walk back to the small ferry pier by the same path or along Peak Road which follows the ridge.

Appendix 1

MUSEUMS OF CHINESE HERITAGE

Flagstaff House, Museum of Tea Ware
Hong Kong Park, Cotton Tree Drive
Tel: 2869 0690

Opening hours
Daily 10 a.m. to 5 p.m.
Closed on Mondays

Admission free

Fung Ping Shan Museum
University of Hong Kong, Bonham Road, Hong Kong
Tel: 2859 2114

Opening hours
Monday to Saturday: 9 a.m. to 6 p.m.
Closed on Sundays and Public Holidays

Admission free

Hong Kong Museum of Art
10 Salisbury Road, Tsim Sha Tsui, Kowloon
Tel: 2734 2136

Opening hours
Monday to Saturday: 10 a.m. to 6 p.m.;
Sundays and Public Holidays: 1 p.m. to 6 p.m.
Closed on Mondays

Admission $10

Hong Kong Museum of History
Kowloon Park, Haiphong Road, Kowloon
Tel: 2367 1124

Opening hours
Monday to Saturday: 10 a.m. to 6 p.m.;
Sundays and Public Holidays: 1 p.m. to 6 p.m.
Closed on Mondays

Admission $10

Hong Kong Museum of Medical Science
2 Caine Lane, Mid-Levels, Hong Kong
Tel: 2549 9458

Opening hours
Monday to Saturday: 10 a.m. to 5 p.m.
Sundays: 1 a.m. to 5 p.m.
Closed on Mondays

Admission free

The Hong Kong Railway Museum
On Fu Road, Tai Po
Tel: 2653 3339

Opening hours
Daily (including Sundays and Public
Holidays) 9 a.m. to 5 p.m.
Closed on Tuesdays, Christmas Day,
Boxing Day, New Year's Day and the
first three days of Lunar New Year Day

Admission free

Law Uk Folk Museum
14 Kut Shing Street, Chai Wan, Hong
Kong
Tel: 2896 7006

Opening hours
Monday to Saturday: 10 a.m. to 1 p.m.;
2 p.m. to 6 p.m. Sundays and Public
Holidays: 1 p.m. to 6 p.m.
Closed on Mondays

Admission free

**Lei Cheng Uk, Tomb of the Han
Dynasty**
41, Tonkin Street, Sham Shui Po,
Kowloon
Tel: 2386 7006

Opening hours
Monday to Saturday: 10 a.m. to 1 p.m.;
2 p.m. to 6 p.m. Sundays and Public
Holidays: 12 p.m. to 6 p.m.
Closed on Mondays

Admission free

Lions Nature Education Centre
Hiram's Highway, Sai Kung
Tel: 2792 2234

Opening hours
Daily 9.30 a.m. to 5 p.m.
Closed on Tuesdays

Admission free

Sam Tung Uk Museum
Kwu Uk Lane, Tsuen Wan
Tel: 2411 2001

Opening hours
Daily (including Sundays and Public
Holidays) 9 a.m. to 4 p.m.
Closed on Tuesdays, Christmas Day,
Boxing Day, New Year's Day and the
first three days of Lunar New Year.

Admission free

Sheung Yiu Folk Museum
Pak Tam Chung Nature Trail, Sai Kung
Tel: 2792 6365

Opening hours
Daily (including Sundays and Public
Holidays) 9 a.m. to 4 p.m.
Closed on Tuesdays, Christmas Day,
Boxing Day, New Year's Day and the
first three days of Lunar New Year

Admission free

The Tsui Museum of Art
11th Floor, Bank of China Building, 2A,
De Voeux Road, Central, Hong Kong
Tel: 2868 2688

Opening hours
Monday to Friday: 10 a.m. to 6 p.m.
Saturday: 10 a.m. to 2 p.m.
Closed on Sundays and Public Holidays

Admission $30

Appendix 2

DECLARED PUBLIC MONUMENTS
New Territories and Outlying islands

Forts
Tung Chung Fort, Lantau
Tung Chung Battery, Lantau
Fan Lau Fort, Lantau

Villages
Kat Hing Wai walled village, Kam Tin
Kun Lung (Sai Wai) walled village and
  gate tower
Ma Wat Wai entrance tower, Lung
  Yeuk Tau, Fanling
Lo Wai, Lung Yeuk Tau, Fanling
Sam Tung Uk village, Tsuen Wan
Sheung Yiu Folk Museum, Pak Tam
  Chung, Sai Kung

Houses
Law Uk, Chai Wan, Hong Kong
The Old House, Hoi Pa Garden, Tsuen
  Wan
Tai Fu Tai, San Tin

Temples
Hung Shing Temple, Wan Chai
I Shing King Temple, Wang Chau, Yuen
  Long
Man Mo Temple, Tai Po
Yeung Hau Temple, Tung Tau Tsuen,
  Yuen Long

Ancestral Halls
Cheung Chun Yuen, Kam Tin
Hau Kui Shek Tong, Ho Sheung Heung,
  Sheung Shui
Man Lung Fung Tong, San Tin
Liu Man Shek Tong, Sheung Shui
Loi Shing Tong, Kam Tin
Tang Chung Ling Tong, Lung Yeuk Tau,
  Fanling
Yiu Kiu Tong, Ping Shan

Study Halls
Kang Yung Shu Uk, Sheung Wo Hang,
  Sha Tau Kok
Kun Ting Study Hall, Ping Shan
Yi Tai Shu Yuen, Kam Tin
Shut Hing study hall entrance, Ping
  Shan

Others
Old Tai Po Market Railway Station
Remains of the Pottery Kilns, Wun Yiu,
  Tai Po
Tsui Shing Lau Pagoda, Ping Shan

Bibliography

Baker, Hugh, *Chinese Family and Kinship*, Columbia, NY: Columbia University Press, 1979

Baker, Hugh, Ancestral Images, Hong Kong: South China Morning Post Ltd, 1979

——, More Ancestral Images, Hong Kong: South China Morning Post Ltd, 1980

——, Ancestral Images Again, Hong Kong: South China Morning Post Ltd, 1981

Bard, Solomon, *In Search of the Past: A Guide to the Antiquities of Hong Kong*, Hong Kong: The Urban Council, 1988

Barnes, Cary F., The Richard Wilhelm translation of *I Ching, The Book of Changes*, London: Routledge & Kegan Paul Ltd, 1951

Blyth, Sally and Ian Wotherspoon, *Hong Kong Remembers*, Hong Kong: Oxford University Press, 1996

Bourton, P. D. W. (ed.), *The Heritage of Hong Kong*, Hong Kong: Antiquities and Monuments Office, 1992

Burkhardt, V. R., *Chinese Creeds and Customs*, Volumes I, II, and III, Hong Kong: South China Morning Post Ltd, 1953–8

Cheung Siu-cheong and Li Ning-hon (eds.), *Chinese Medicinal Herbs of Hong Kong*, Volumes 1–7, Hong Kong: Commercial Press 1991–7

Cheung, S. T. *Fortune Stick Predictions: Man Mo Temple*, Hong Kong: Board of Directors, Tung Wah Group of Hospitals, 1981

Christian, Jochim, *Chinese Religions: A Cultural Perspective*, New Jersey: Prentice Hall, 1986

Chamberlain, Jonathan, *Chinese Gods*, Malaysia: Peklanduk Publications, 1987

Ching, Julia, *Chinese Religions*, London: Macmillan, 1993

Cumine, Eric, *Hong Kong Ways and Byways*, Hong Kong: Belongers Publications Ltd, 1981

Dwyer Ball, J., *Things Chinese*, Shanghai: Kelly & Walsh, 1925

Eberhard, Wolfram, *Times Dictionary of Chinese Symbols*, Federal Publications 1983

Faure, David; Hayes, James; and Birch, Alan (eds), *From Village to City*, Hong Kong: Centre of Asian Studies, University of Hong Kong, 1984

Harz, Paula R., *Taoism*, New York: Facts On File, Inc., 1993

Hase, Patrick and Sinn, Elizabeth, *Beyond the Metropolis: Villages in Hong Kong*, Hong Kong: Joint Publishing Co. Ltd, 1995

Hayes, James, *The Rural Communities of Hong Kong: Studies and Themes*, Hong Kong: Nordica Printing Co., 1983

Hayes, James, *The Hong Kong Region, 1850–1911*, Connecticut: Archon Books, 1977

Ho Puay Peng, *The Living Building: Vernacular Environments of South China*, Hong Kong, Chinese University Press, 1995

Hoobler, Thomas and Dorothy, *Confucianism*, New York: Facts On File, Inc., 1993

Hong Kong Historical Society, *Forts and Pirates*, 1990

Hong Kong Government Information Services, *Rural Architecture in Hong Kong*, 1979

Hu Dongshu, *The Way of the Virtuous: The Influence of Art and Philosophy on Chinese Garden Design*, New World Press, 1991

Keswick, Maggie, *The Chinese Garden*, London: St Martin's Press, 1986

Knapp, Ronald. G., *The Chinese House*, Hong Kong: Oxford University Press, 1990

Lam Kam-Chuen, *The Feng Shui Handbook*, London: Gala Books Ltd, 1995

Lau, T. C., *The Eight Immortals*, Hong Kong: Wing Tai Cheung Printing Co. Ltd, 1972

Lang, Graeme and Ragvald, Lars, *The Rise of a Refugee God: Hong Kong's Wong Tai Sin*, Hong Kong: Oxford University Press, 1993

Law, Joan, and Wars, Barbara, *Chinese Festivals*, Hong Kong: South China Post Ltd, 1982

Lip, Evelyn, *Chinese Temples and Deities*, Singapore: Times Books International, 1953

Lo Hsiang-lin, et al., *Hong Kong and its External Communications before 1842*, Hong Kong: Institute of Culture, 1963

Lowenstein, Tom, *The Vision of Buddha*, London: Macmillan, 1996

Lye Eric K. C. (ed), *Chinese Traditional Architecture*, Hong Kong, The Regional Council, 1991

Man Ho Kwok; Palmer, Martin; and Ramsay, Jay, *Tao Te Ching*, Element Books Ltd, 1994

Maryknoll Mission, *Letters from China*, London: Macmillan, 1927

Overmyer, Daniel L. *Religions of China*, London: HarperCollins Publishers, 1985

Palmer, Martin, *Travels through Sacred China*, London: Thorsons, 1996

Palmer, Martin, *The Elements of Taoism*, Shaftsbury, Dorset: Element Books Ltd, 1991

Rawson, Jessica (ed), *Mysteries of Ancient China: New Discoveries from the Early Dynasties*, London: British Museum Press, 1996

Regional Council of Hong Kong, *From Study Hall to Village School*, 1996

Reid, Daniel P., *Chinese Herbal Medicine*, CFW Publications Ltd, 1987

Rodwell, Sally, *Historic Hong Kong: A Visitor's Guide*, Hong Kong, The Guidebook Company, 1991

Sacred Symbols: Tao, London: Thames and Hudson, 1996

Savidge, Joyce, *This is Hong Kong: Temples*, Hong Kong Information Services, 1977

Smith, Richard J., *Chinese Almanacs*, Hong Kong: Oxford University Press, 1992

Snelling, John, *Buddhism: A Richly Illustrated Voyage into the Heart of the Buddhist Tradition*, Shaftsbury, Dorset: Element Books Ltd, 1996

Ting, Joseph S. P., and Siu, Susanna L. K. (eds.), *Collected Essays on Various Historical Materials for Hong Kong Studies*, Hong Kong: The Urban Council, 1990

Transport Department, *Public Transport in Hong Kong: A Guide to Services in 1996*, Hong Kong: Hong Kong Transport Department, 1996

Waley, Arthur, *170 Chinese Poems*, London: Constable and Co. Ltd, 1918

Waley, Arthur, *Chinese Poems*, London: Allen and Unwin, 1949

Walters Dr D., *Faces of Hong Kong: An Old Hand's Reflections*, Singapore: Prentice Hall 1995

Wangu Madhu Bazaz, *Buddhism*, New York: Facts On File, Inc., 1993

Wang Ying-lin (trans. Xu Chui-yang), *The Three Character Classic in Comics*, Singapore: EPB Publishers Pte Ltd, 1993

Williams C. A. S., *Outlines of Chinese Symbolism and Art Motives*, London: Dover Publications 1976

Index

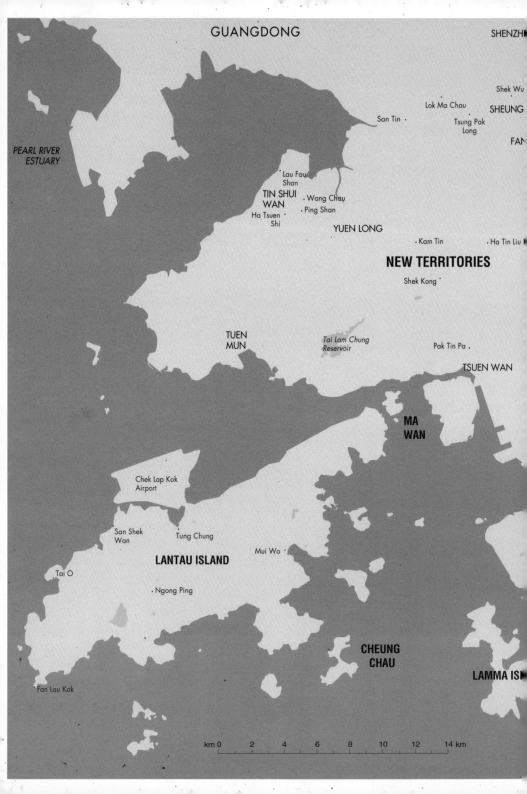